"Hansen peels off the skin of ministry and cuts to its core, forcing the reader to ask, 'Do I really love the church I serve?'"

—Eugene Peterson

"Out of the tender strength of his own experience of weakness, Dave Hansen wonderfully teaches and encourages pastors to love that often most unlovable bride, the church."

—Michael Card

"Here's to tough thinking and sensitivity, to vision and need! Here's to Dave Hansen, who often questions himself on the way to a great failure. Read and walk with him."

—Calvin Miller

"David Hansen loves Jesus Christ, and he loves the church of Jesus Christ. He tells how all pastors can become church lovers. He teaches us to lead with love."

—Leith Anderson

The Power of
Loving Your Church

PASTOR'S SOUL SERIES
David L. Goetz, General Editor

The Power of Loving Your Church
David Hansen

Pastoral Grit
Craig Brian Larson

LIBRARY OF LEADERSHIP DEVELOPMENT
Marshall Shelley, General Editor

Leading Your Church Through Conflict and Reconciliation
Renewing Your Church Through Vision and Planning
Building Your Church Through Counsel and Care
Growing Your Church Through Training and Motivation

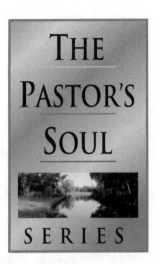

THE
PASTOR'S
SOUL

SERIES

The Power of
Loving Your Church

DAVID·HANSEN

David L. Goetz · General Editor

BETHANY HOUSE PUBLISHERS
MINNEAPOLIS, MINNESOTA 55438

Published by Bethany House Publishers
A Ministry of Bethany Fellowship, Inc.
11300 Hampshire Avenue South
Minneapolis, Minnesota 55438

Printed in the United States of America by
Bethany Press International, Minneapolis, Minnesota 55438

Library of Congress Cataloging-in-Publication Data

Hansen, David, 1953–
    The power of loving your church : leading through acceptance and grace / by David Hansen.
        p. cm. — (The pastor's soul series)
    ISBN 1–55661–968–5
    1. Pastoral theology. 2. Church. I. Title. II. Series.
BV4011.H333   1997
253—dc21   97–33847
                                                               CIP

DAVID HANSEN is pastor of Belgrade Community Church in Belgrade, Montana. He is a popular LEADERSHIP columnist and author of *The Art of Pastoring* and *A Little Handbook on Having a Soul*.

DAVID L. GOETZ is senior associate editor of LEADERSHIP, a publication of Christianity Today, Inc.

ACKNOWLEDGMENTS

IN MANY WAYS this book was born on a trout stream. LEADERSHIP senior associate editor Dave Goetz raised the idea of writing a book while we were fly-fishing the Madison River near my home in Montana in March 1996, in a snowstorm. We frosted some brain cells that day, caught a lot of fish (Dave caught more than I did), and we came up with an idea for a book.

Except for getting out-fished, that's one awfully fine definition of a good day.

Furthermore, the material for this book came from hundreds of hours on trout streams, wandering, praying, and struggling for answers to the perpetual conundrum called pastoral ministry. Only long prayer provides the answers. Time and time again, when I wanted to lash out at my congregation, raise my fist against God and quit, the solution came in one word: love.

Love is not the easy answer. It is the toughest possible answer, and it requires more time alone, wandering and praying, to figure out what it means to love God, to love a congregation, and have a little respect left over for yourself. I have discovered I am not alone in my questions about what love means to pastoral ministry.

The specifics of this book evolved from visits with pastors about the issue of love in ministry. The publication of my first book, *The Art of Pastoring: Ministry Without All the Answers*, brought with it requests to meet with pastors. In these seminars, whenever the subject of pastoral love came up, interest piqued and tough questions popped up like dandelions. These conversations helped me develop the themes of this book. I am extremely grateful for chances to meet with American Baptist pastors in Montana; North Puget Sound, Washington; Wichita, Kansas; and the Dakotas. I also want to express thanks to Bethel Seminary and the Ockenga Institute at Gordon-Conwell Theological Seminary for opportunities to share portions of this material with pastors, students, and faculty.

I wish to thank Dave Goetz at LEADERSHIP for giving me the opportunity to write this book, for his constant encouragement during writing, and for his final edit of the book. Special thanks go to The Reverend Patricia Duckworth, area minister for the American Baptist Churches, Big Sky Area, Montana, to my son, Evan Hansen, for reading the manuscript and for offering many helpful suggestions, and to the Reverend Rusty Strickler, pastor of Crow Community Church, Crow Agency, Montana.

Finally, beyond question, my greatest resource for what love means to pastoral ministry came from the genuine, caring servants of Christ who have pastored me over many years. In all of my rambling, wandering prayers, I found myself, again and again, asking the Lord how I could do what *they* did. I wish to thank the following pastors for demonstrating in life what I have reproduced poorly in print: George Munzing, Bob Cahill, Tom Elson, and Gordon Hugenberger.

Of these great men, I do not hesitate to isolate one. I dedicate this book to The Reverend George A. Munzing, pastor of Trinity United Presbyterian Church, Santa Ana, California, from 1959 to 1997. During his ministry, more than ninety men and women responded to God's call to ministry and missions. In the thirty years I have known him as pastor, head of staff, and friend, George has demonstrated steadfast love, compassion, friendship, and sacrifice, not only consistently—which is amazing enough— but increasingly.

In my long walks, trying to figure things out, I often asked myself, "What would George do?" The answer comes in his voice and through the testimony of his life: "Do the right thing, the loving thing. People before programs. Faithfulness to Christ above all."

CONTENTS

FOREWORD

"PASTORAL WORK HAS fundamentally changed. Today it's harder, more complex, more intense than it was in generations past. The church needs to be reengineered to become a cultural force; pastors must look to new paradigms for their calling and see their role in fresh ways."

So proclaim many ministry pundits these days.

Can that be fully true? At its center, is the nature of pastoral work today discontinuous with how pastors have practiced their calling for two thousand years?

While $100,000 tractors have replaced plow horses, modern farmers still farm. The center of what they do remains: to work the land to produce a crop. And modern pastors still pastor. The frontier of the twenty-first century may require new ministry methods, but the core task of cultivating souls demands men and women who understand the nature of their fundamental calling.

That's why the editors of LEADERSHIP, a practical journal devoted to helping pastors be more faithful and effective, have developed THE PASTOR'S SOUL book series. The phrase *pastor's soul* is used here in a metaphorical sense, denoting that which is central to the work of a pastor. While some pastors use PowerPoint℗, video clips, and sophisticated drama in Sunday morning worship, and others still make house calls, the center of the pastoral task remains: to make saints by calling people to worship and service.

The Power of Loving Your Church: Leading Through Acceptance and Grace is the first volume in this eight-book lineup. Montana pastor Dave Hansen examines the four pastoral loves, which form the bedrock for leading the saints. Future volumes in the series will highlight prayer, character, preaching, calling, and spirituality—all part of the center of pastoral work. Several of LEADERSHIP's most influential contributors—including Kent Hughes, Ben Patterson, and Fred Smith—will address these issues in forthcoming books.

Our desire is that THE PASTOR's SOUL series will dignify the calling of pastors and provide realistic help for its central tasks.

—David L. Goetz
General Editor

INTRODUCTION

IN LATIN THE WORD *pastor* means "shepherd" or "herdsman." The word is derived from the Latin word *pascere*, which means "to pasture" or "to feed."

Ancient cultures valued shepherds differently. Whereas Egyptian and Greco-Roman high culture despised shepherds as low-class trash, the biblical tradition honored shepherds: Abraham was a shepherd. Israel takes its name from Abraham's grandson Jacob, a shrewd shepherd and a potent father. Moses couldn't lead Israel until he'd paid his dues as a shepherd. David, Israel's great warrior/poet king, began his life as a shepherd and never forgot it. He slew Goliath with a strategy learned in shepherding. He fixed shepherding into biblical tradition forever by writing Psalm 23, in which he calls God a shepherd and makes shepherding out to be something nearly divine. The prophet Nathan used David's love of shepherding against him when he skewered David with a parable about a poor shepherd and a wealthy rancher. The prophet Ezekiel demanded that Israel's corrupt religious professionals become like good shepherds or face the consequences.

Jesus, furthermore, utilized the tradition of the good shepherd in his teaching. He told the parable of the good shepherd that left the flock to seek the lost lamb. He revealed the nature of his ministry and his divinity in the metaphor of the good shepherd. After his resurrection Jesus rehearsed Peter's three denials with three questions about whether Peter loved him or not. Jesus followed Peter's guilty, pained confession of love with the demand: "feed my sheep" (John 21:15).

From David on, the biblical tradition is clear: good shepherds love their flock, God loves his flock, and God's leaders must love their flock. Following the Scriptures, church tradition is unequivocal: good pastors love their flock, bad pastors do not love their flock.

When a church and its parishioners are easy to love, the admonition seems superfluous. Every pastor wants to love his or her church. But not all churches are easy to love, and not all pastors find love easy, and the two have uncanny ways of finding each other.

So most of us pastors need to learn how to love our church. We need to learn to love our church because it is hard to love and because we are hard to love, and if we don't figure out how to love our church, it's curtains for our call to pastoral work.

This book is more about learning to love our church than it is about learning to love our people. For instance, it is not about learning to love difficult parishioners. Other contemporary books, such as Marshall Shelley's *Well-Intentioned Dragons*, deal with that issue well. Of course I've served a few well-intentioned dragons. You might say this book is about learning to love the well-intentioned dragon's lair.

This book is about our need to love our whole church. That is, we need to love the institutional church we serve including its past, present, and future. We need to love the people of the church not just as individuals but as a family system. We need to learn to love the buildings, the programs, the trees, and the shrubs (all in proper order, of course!).

Why?

Because God loves the people of our church as a family of believers. And because God cares about the buildings and the programs and the trees and the shrubs. After all, they were given to him.

One assumption of this book is that some churches are hard to love and that as pastors we can do better at learning how to love them. Though this thesis requires little substantiation, it definitely requires elucidation. Tough churches perplex us, especially when, as in the case of those I have served, they are made up of fine, genuine Christians. Though the individuals cared for me and I for them, corporately the churches acted like a mother grizzly with cubs. I often stumbled between the mother and her cubs. The cubs were the church's grudges.

Typically the bewilderment we feel as pastors when the people love us but the church tears us apart is also felt by church members, who cannot figure out why their church can't break out of decades-long failure cycles. They feel shame. They can't figure out why they beat up pastors, like a parent feels after he beats up his kid again—and doesn't know why or how to stop.

Rationalization covers the shame. These well-meaning people simply have bad luck with pastors.

Early in my second year of a pastorate, a parishioner recounted for me the church's thirty-year struggle with pastors. After thirty minutes of listening, I asked her, "I admit there are some pastors who don't know what they are doing, but did it ever occur to you that the church might be just a little bit at fault too?"

"No," she said; the thought had never crossed her mind.

To put the situation differently, how is it possible for a ruling board of twelve kind, Christ-honoring human beings—all of whom have fine, adult intelligence—to make decisions about the way they treat their pastors consistently reflecting a corporate IQ of about 80?

This is not only possible, it is *likely* if the church is held in a headlock by old fights, desperate insecurities, and the odious task of calling a new pastor every three years. Fear and resentment always retard common sense. *A church that cannot incarnate corporately the gifts and values held by its individual members is hard to love.*

For example, a church whose corporate psyche is covertly obsessed with grudges may not be able to keep the church property in good shape. Here's what's happening:

(1) the members value living in tidy homes, implying that,

(2) they should want their church/parsonage to reflect that value, but,

(3) because of overt and covert church fights, they are powerless to apply their own strongly held

values to something as simple as replacing some linoleum.

Imagine trying to accomplish something as challenging as evangelism and integrating new members into such a church!

Pastors in these churches feel like children caught in vicious custody battles:

- "Why can't they get anything done without fighting?"
- "They say they love me. Why can't they get along?"
- "This must be my fault."
- "If I'm a good boy, everything will be better."

Churches like this need strong love. But not only for the individuals, because love for individuals may be interpreted as taking sides! To heal the church, the pastor must learn to love the *whole* church.

I knew it before I wrote this book, but not nearly as severely as I know it now: Love is dangerous. And it is dangerous to write about love. If you write about love triumphantly, love makes you into a hypocrite. If you write about love skeptically, loves makes you into a whiner. Undoubtedly in places in this book I have stepped over both lines.

But a book about love may also be dangerous to its readers. Love pushes us to desperate measures. A book on love taken seriously by a well-meaning pastor may make him or her even more vulnerable to the unconscionable abuse a church can mete out. The other threat is much different: Pastoral love is dangerous because it can manipulate parishioners sexually. *Eros,* obviously, is not included in the four great loves of pastoral ministry, but these four loves can cause sexual arousal in some people.

For these reasons, I strongly urge the reader to read the entire book before drawing any firm conclusions about the role of love in pastoral ministry. Chapters seven, eight, and nine discuss the importance of knowing how and when to walk away from pastor-killing churches, how to pray for unlovable churches, and the unscrupulous role of *eros* in pastoral ministry.

We've all been burned by love. Each of us fears it. Some pastors give up on it. And yet we all know that love is essential to pastoral ministry. To help us reclaim love we need to answer questions like: What kinds of love are essential to ministry? What do different kinds of love accomplish? How do we get past the obstacles to love?

I don't say much in the book about the awful chore my churches faced in learning to love me, their pastor. I assure you my part was not more challenging than theirs. At every step we deserved each other. What we never deserved was the love Christ gave us for one another, a love that, in fits and starts, we yielded to.

We definitely serve a patient, patient Lord.

1

THE BALL-CAP CRISIS

ONE CAN NEVER KNOW how delicately balanced a long-term truce is until its equilibrium is shattered by the weight of a straw, a straw that lands as if it were a ten-pound hammer.

In a church I served, the straw was a few kids wearing ball caps in the worship service.

The church was a hundred years old in a town barely older. Both showed their age. But the town and the church stood as landmarks of human determination to beat a living out of poor soil and bad weather. These people were tough. They put up with a lot to live there, and generally they put up with a lot from each other. Their main prejudice was against disingenuousness. The rule was, "Don't act like one of us if you ain't." People who moved in and right away bought fancy western clothes didn't last long.

I grew up in big cities and preached in a dark gray suit that would have worked in Boston. Yet it was not uncommon when calling on older people in the congregation—lifelong, cow-punching Montanans—for them to say to me, "You're just like one of our kids." I didn't look like their kids, I didn't talk like their kids, but apparently there was something about me that reflected the place's ethos more deeply than clothing or language.

I learned that I could talk about things they talked about only if I knew something about what they were talking about; otherwise, I should ask polite questions or keep my mouth shut. Once they figured out I was a good fly-fisherman, they enjoyed sermon illustrations from fishing, but I never tried illustrations from hunting.

I learned about my new culture's antipathy toward disingenuousness at a potluck supper following my candidating sermon. I was sitting at a table with several men who started talking about chain saws. I offered some opinions about the nasty beasts. One of the men in the group glared at me, laughed, and said, "Hey, listen to the preacher talk about chain saws."

I answered his challenge with a simple statement of the truth: "I cut and sold twelve cords of firewood to pay for my chain saw, and I've cut wood to heat our home for the last three winters."

"Then you do know what you're talking about," he said. He was pleased with my answer, and I rejoined the conversation on equal terms; he and I remained on excellent terms.

Through the years, the insight held up: People didn't care who moved in, where they were from, what they did, how they dressed, or how they talked as long as it was genuine. Sexism wasn't nearly as big a prob-

lem here as I'd seen it in more urbane areas of the
country. In this town the women had worked side by
side with the men for generations simply for survival.
Our congressional district elected the first woman to
Congress, Jeanette Rankin. She distinguished herself
by being the only member of Congress to vote against
entering World War I and World War II.

So when some home-grown high school kids
took the Sunday morning offering wearing cut-off
sweat pants and T-shirts ripped halfway up, no one
said a thing. It was football clothing. High school
sports is god in little Montana towns, so even though
the dress seemed inappropriate, wearing football re-
galia made cultural sense. It made us feel proud to be
so open to high school kids. Looking back, I think we
were affirming football, not openness to kids.

The parents of the boys thought the whole thing
was great; so did I. So when the mom, the church pi-
anist, came to me one Sunday morning right before
the service and said, "I hope you don't mind if the
boys wear hats in church today. They got in late from
the game last night, and they didn't wake up in time
to take showers, so their hair is all messed up," I
shrugged my shoulders. Montana schools are so far
apart that it is not uncommon for teams to travel six
hours to a contest. The boys hadn't gotten in until
3:30 in the morning. A lot of kids in athletics don't
make it to church at all during the sports seasons; I
figured it was better to have them in church with caps
on than not at all. I respected the family's desire for
the boys to be in church.

Thinking back on what they'd worn in the past,

I said to their mom, "I don't see why it should be a problem."

When I entered the sanctuary, I saw the boys—wearing nice clothes and ball caps. The service went fine, and I didn't hear a word from anyone about it. Naturally, the boys wore their caps in church the next week and the next.... It took a month before the sheep began to bleat:

"I wish the boys wouldn't wear hats in church."

"Pastor, do you think the boys should be wearing hats in church?"

I consistently defended the boys with passive responses: "It's just good to have them in church. Hats aren't such a big deal." That would end the conversation.

This pattern continued for about four months. In the early stages, we probably thought the ball-cap issue was nothing but a rough spot that would smooth out. Though the church (and the town) barely survived bitter fights in the '60s and '70s, during my nine years of ministry we enjoyed growth and peace. We knew "how very good and pleasant it is when kindred live together in unity!" (Ps. 133:1). We thought the days of mistrust and division were over. We saw nothing but blue skies and good times ahead, while pockets of resentment stacked up like heaps of dry tinder around our feet. The steel struck the flint in an unexpected way.

Killing frost

It was a clear, cool Sunday morning in July. The sun warmed the earth and the water in the Bitterroot

River as the congregation gathered for worship, anticipating our annual river baptism and potluck picnic afterward. While the rest of the nation steamed and sweated, we enjoyed our typical cool evenings and warm days with low humidity, hoping against hope that our tomatoes would ripen before the killing frost around Labor Day. I suppose the biggest thing on most of our minds was potato salad.

While I was in the back room with the accompanists, making last-minute preparations for worship, a man in his mid-twenties, an East Coast out-of-towner with a shaggy mane and a fast motorcycle, walked from the rear of the sanctuary where he was seated to the front where the boys were seated. He asked them to remove their hats out of respect for the house of God.

This man, who attended worship regularly, was loved by everyone. I called him "Twinkie Man" because he distributed Hostess products to valley grocers to support himself as he pursued graduate studies at the University of Montana.

The boys, unaccustomed to taking orders from anyone, refused. He insisted. They balked. The stepfather of one of the boys came up and silently placed his own hat on his head and sat by the boys. This ended the confrontation.

When I entered the sanctuary seconds later, I noticed the dad sitting next to the boys wearing a cap. I didn't think much of it. The service went as usual. I thought the sermon was pretty good, but I realize now that no one was listening. At the end of the service, as the boys' parents came through the line, they said, "The boys shouldn't have been treated that way," as if I knew what had happened.

The stepfather, who had pulled off ball-cap solidarity resistance, said essentially the same thing and mentioned something about the guy who'd perpetrated the injustice. Others said, "We're glad the young man confronted them." So when the Twinkie Man came by, I asked if we could talk.

He told me what he'd done, and I was mad at him for it. I defended the boys' right to wear hats in church. He said it wasn't right for the boys to wear hats in the house of God, especially since their doing so offended older members. I told him I didn't think they had offended anyone. He disagreed.

I still believed the situation would resolve itself. After all, the church had shown itself open to many people—they loved the Twinkie Man. The boys were from a key family in the church. Why wouldn't the little game eventually lose inertia? Didn't we all love each other?

Hats of rebellion

The next week the comments against the ball caps started coming in like high-and-tight fastballs. So I wrote a letter to the congregation. I defended the boys' right to wear hats in church from Paul's letter to the Galatian church. From my perspective the boys were simply exercising their freedom in Christ. I thought about Paul's admonition to the Corinthian church not to offend fellow Christians and the importance of not making the gospel incomprehensible to local culture, but I dismissed it. I was in the mood to be a hero, and I was afraid of the family. If that sounds like a contradiction, it is; I thought if the church could cut the kids a little New Testament slack, everything would settle down.

As I reread that letter today, it sounds like NRA or ACLU rhetoric. The substance of my letter went as follows:

> *Do we really want to go back to dress codes? Where will it end? If we start to take away people's freedom about something like a hat, what about when people start demanding that women wear dresses? Or that men must wear coats and ties? Don't laugh. If we take away freedom and begin with dress codes, where will it end?*
>
> *We can't let an issue like hats in worship divide this church and stop our work; the times are too dangerous, Christian faith is too rare, churches around us are dying, and people in our community (some of whom wear ball caps) need to hear the Good News. After all, someday the kid who comes to church with a ball cap eager to hear the gospel might be your child or your grandchild.*

The congregation said little about the letter. One man, whom I'd baptized in the Bitterroot River with his cowboy boots on, had the guts to come to me and explain that for a man to wear a hat in church just wasn't right. I ignored him. Of course the boys' families loved the letter. A family member said, "Thanks for taking our side." That should have clued me in that something deeper was going on. But the worst of it was, I was disingenuous. I was spouting off self-righteously, but I didn't know what I was talking about. I had seriously misjudged the congregational, cultural, and pastoral dynamics of the situation.

The Twinkie Man knew, as I did not, that to this culture, wearing hats in worship wasn't simply a matter of personal discretion, it was a matter of the profanation of worship. The men in the community wore hats in restaurants, in their homes, at dinner, and at school concerts, but when the flag was presented, the hats came off. I should have remembered that. They wore their hats at graveside services, until we prayed, and then the hats came off. When they walked into a church building, the hats came off.

For your basic rancher, a hat is a sign of independence and even a little rebellion. Often men wear hats at school concerts because for the most part they dislike school concerts. They wear hats at restaurants to be rascals. But when the flag goes by or someone starts praying or they walk into a church, their hats come off as a sign of submission to a higher authority. Wearing a hat in church was deeply offensive to these people.

The boys were vaguely aware that hats were a sign of rebellion. The parents knew it acutely. For the boys the hats were fashionable. They definitely enjoyed stirring things up a bit, but they'd been doing it for years in the church, and we'd let them. They were rascals in a culture that rewarded rascalism. For the parents, particularly the mother, the hats symbolized a power struggle that had been going on in the church for decades. I didn't see it because I didn't want to. The family had been dear to me through tough funerals and joyous baptisms. I'd baptized the boys in the Bitterroot River. Through hours of talking over coffee and working shoulder to shoulder in ministry, I had become part of the extended family that included Grandma and some aunts and uncles. I did not want to lose these relationships, but I was being edged toward tough decisions: What would I do if I had to decide between the family and the church? What would happen to me?

The issue became a crisis. No one called special meetings, no one talked about a church split, the Twinkie Man cooled his engine, but the tension in the fellowship was overwhelming. When we gathered for worship, fellowship, or business, it was as if we were walking barefoot on shattered glass, smiling through the tears; no one wanted to admit that it hurt. I felt I needed to act in a decisive way, so I went and made the worst pastoral visit of my life.

I went alone to meet with the family of two of the boys. I had no clear idea of what I wanted to accomplish. I didn't understand the issues. I went with so much cognitive dissonance and emotional pain that I was ready to accept any settlement that offered me relief. It is obvious to me now that I set myself up to cave in. After a long discussion in which I pretended to talk tough, I agreed that the boys should make their own decision about whether they would wear their caps in church. The mother had insisted the boys be allowed to make their own decision. I should have realized that this was her battle.

How could I have put a decision, upon which the

future of the church depended, into the hands of two high school kids? It was too much responsibility for them and so much irresponsibility from me. Of course the boys did not remove their hats.

Did I pray? Constantly. For hours. For answers. For wisdom. For mercy. For resolution. For anesthesia. But nothing came of it.

I was not to be allowed under any circumstances to come away from this debacle as the hero. God wasn't leading me; he was using me. He was using the family and the church. I had some things to learn that only something this painful and befuddling could teach me.

Finally I asked for advice outside of the community.

Eruption

I telephoned two veteran pastors, each twenty years ahead of me, each a mentor. Neither knew the other, but their conclusions were unanimous, and their words bore uncanny similarity: "You need to save the church. Go to the boys privately and ask them to remove their hats. They will respect your authority."

I knew they were right, but I knew it was risky. I was going back on my previous stance, though I was willing to admit that I had been wrong. I knew what it really meant was that I had to choose the church over the family. My battle-toughened friends knew this, and they knew I needed to do it. This raised a primary issue that my first twelve years of pastoral ministry had not forced me to deal with: *Do I pastor a church, or do I pastor a collection of individuals?*

My theology told me that I pastor a church. I believed the church is more important than its pastor or its individual members. But my heart always told me that I pastor individuals. I figured that if I loved the individuals in the church sufficiently, loving the church would take care of itself.

For the most part, my pact with my heart worked pretty well. But this was the school of hard knocks, and my inner agreement was not up to the demands of reality.

So I went to the boys when I knew their parents weren't home and asked the boys if they would remove their caps for the sake of the church. They readily agreed. And they seemed relieved. I returned from the meeting exultant. I could see the solution taking shape: The boys remove their caps, and they get the credit for doing the right thing. It seemed perfect.

Instead, it was like the decapitation of Mount St. Helens, which erupted in my face the next morning.

Of course the boys told their parents, and of course Mom and Dad blew sky high. The process that followed was thoroughly unpleasant and nothing but heartbreaking to the bitter end. Amazingly, during the final period of the conflict, the church was largely silent. They knew what I'd done, and they respected me for it. They didn't taunt or push or even encourage. They just watched and prayed. None of the council members forced me to choose between their opinion and the church. At the final, crucial council meeting, several council members stood up for what I'd done.

One of them, a young man, spoke words I will not forget: "I will admit that I did not like seeing caps in church. But you are our leader, and I was willing to follow your call. You had the right to talk to the boys alone because you are their pastor, like a coach has the right to talk to his ball players. You have made the call, and we need to stand by it. I agree with what you have done. I respect you for taking a stand. I'm with you."

That was all that needed to be said. It still amazes me that the council would have followed my lead whatever stand I took. The family, on the other hand, could abide with only one solution—theirs. No matter how tortuous and bumpy my road to the solution was, I know now—and I knew then—that I made the right call.

Ultimately, the whole extended family left the church, nine souls in all. At the time, they represented about 15 percent of our worship attendance. Within two weeks, the positions they held in the church were filled. The place began to grow like never before.

It's not difficult to discern significant errors in my management of the ball-cap crisis.

First, I should never have tried to manage it by myself. I should have handed the issue to the church council early on. The problem was that two of the council members were in the family—including the mom. I assumed the council couldn't deal with it. But I should have let the council struggle over the issue in a fair fight.

Second, I should have recognized how complicated cultural issues are. Before waxing self-righteously about Christian freedom—as if I were the hero
of downtrodden high school kids everywhere—I
should have done my cultural homework. The boys
could have staked their freedom in Christ—as they
already had—without deeply offending the whole
culture around them. I learned it isn't wrong for people to learn courtesy, and it isn't wrong for the church
to require some respect.

Third, I learned how vulnerable I am to entan-
glement in family systems. My little pact with my
heart that I pastor a group of individuals, not a
church, made me especially susceptible. I wasn't prepared to make a decision between dear friends and a
church. The friendship I shared with the family was
real and positive on one level. However, I failed to recognize the church power struggles as one of the forces
binding the family together. I did not realize that as
an adopted member of this family, when a showdown
occurred, I would be expected to side with the family—or reject the family.

Whereas most of the time we can love both the
church and the individuals in it, in this case I was
forced, against my will, to chose which I loved the
most: the church or the family.

Beneath it all, I was being forced to ask whether
I loved the church more than I loved myself. My feelings were being hurt badly, so I didn't want to love
the church. I wanted to love this family. I was required
to side with the church against the family and against
myself.

That decision changed my ministry. I became a stronger pastor. I became a more loving pastor, because I became better able to distinguish between loving people and loving what people do for me. I became a better pastor because it made me decide to love the church.

But what's to love in a church?

Individuals and families are easy to love. But if a situation requires you to love a church over an individual or even an entire family, what is it about a church that you can love? What is there to decide for?

This was the kind of theological/pastoral test only a minimalist context could provide. The numbers were spare, the building was cute (but not that cute), we didn't have children in the nursery, let alone a decent Sunday school or youth ministry. There wasn't a lot to love. That is why it was the perfect test for pastoral theology and pastoral love: Whatever had to be loved about this church must be loved about every church.

It's fairly easy to love the sheer organization of a well-run place or a growing mission program or swarming youth groups or spectacular architecture. But the ball-cap crisis wasn't about despoiling the Cathedral of Notre Dame. My church's primary accomplishment for more than one hundred years was keeping the doors open.

The church had managed to provide weekly, public worship of almighty God for one hundred years. That was it. Perhaps that was all it needed to do. Perhaps it was that very fact that made me choose to love that church over one particular family. For one hundred tough years, that church had been a lampstand, and the risen Christ had been present in its worship:

> Then I turned to see whose voice it was that spoke to me, and on turning I saw seven golden lampstands, and in the midst of the lampstands I saw one like the Son of Man, clothed with a long robe and with a golden sash across his chest. His head and his hair were white as white wool, white as snow; his eyes were like a flame of fire, his feet were like burnished bronze, refined as in a furnace, and his voice was like the sound of many waters. In his right hand he held seven stars, and from his mouth came a sharp, two-edged sword, and his face was like the sun shining with full force. When I saw him, I fell at his feet as though dead. But he placed his right hand on me, saying, "Do not be afraid; I am the first and the last, and the living one. I was dead, and see, I am alive forever and ever; and I have the keys of Death and of Hades. Now write what you have seen, what is, and what is to take place after this. As for the mystery of the seven stars that you saw in my right hand, and the seven golden lampstands: the seven stars are the angels of the seven churches, and the seven lampstands are the seven churches" (Rev. 1:12–20).

No one had the right to disturb or destroy the lampstand. The lampstand was more important than its pastor, its members, or family. I needed to love this lampstand. Anyone can love it with me, but as the pastor I am responsible to respect its past, preserve the integrity of its light in the present, and to ensure that the lampstand has a future.

Even now as I pastor elsewhere, I love that little church more than ever. I love it more than any of its members. Hidden beneath the human foolishness of a church and its pastor as they fumbled their way forward was almighty God.

He sanctifies the individuals, but even more so the church. In this case, the church God planted and preserved is at this time doing better than at any time in its history.

2

WHAT'S LOVE GOT TO DO WITH IT?

THE BALL-CAP CRISIS illustrates the kind of emotional dilemma that kills our pastoral love. Lessons like that stack up pretty fast in ministry. They remind me of the Calvinist who, upon falling down a flight of stairs, shook himself off and declared, "Boy, I'm glad that's over!"

I realize a certain number of debacles are inevitable and that they are good for me. I've tried to learn from my failures, and I think I handle things a little better than I used to. The problem is that though the pain caused by generic human foolishness makes me wiser, it tends to make me ambivalent in my pastoral work.

The word *ambivalence* means "not being able to decide on an issue." Specifically, it means not being able to give ourselves in love, all because of inner pain that shies our will away from any course of action. Ambivalence causes excessive fluctuation on issues, and it can cause an obsession with fluctuation to the point that no decision can be made. Ambivalence is by nature paradoxical. On the one hand, it can cause us to do pastoral work with more than a healthy professional distance. On the other hand, it lowers our natural, healthy defenses and can make us unsure of our personal boundaries. It often causes us to retreat into self-centered self-love as a defense against risking mature, adult love. We become vulnerable to unhealthy forms of love and unhealthy forms of self-sacrifice.

Ambivalence masks itself as wisdom, whispering, "Don't get involved, it only hurts to care. Don't make a decision, someone will be disappointed and you'll have to backtrack...."

This is pseudo-wisdom, leaking into the consciousness from a part of our spirit that refuses to be hurt again; loss, particularly any loss that signals death, is intolerable. Losing my parishioner-friends in the ball-cap crisis ripped my heart out. Not only did it feel like a death, it *was* a kind of death, and I was forced to deal with it as such.

Parents often deal with the death of a child by distancing themselves from the children that remain. This is done as protection from ever being hurt that badly again. Many parents overcome this brutal self-preservation instinct, but it is not easy. Nor is it easy for pastors to override a similar instinct when they lose dear parishioners to conflict. The frequency with which it occurs can build up a reservoir of pain, making pastoral ministry intolerable.

Far-flung cold space

The pain of loss that causes ambivalence can happen to pastors on the corporate level: We feel rejected by the entire church, often through the action of the council. How many times have we heard, "We want to know how you're doing . . . tell us how we can help you," only to find that when we share our tiredness and even illness, we are rebuffed with what amounts to, "We have it worse than you do . . . stop complaining"?

Eight years ago I tried being honest with a church council after being assured that they wanted to know how I was feeling. I got blasted and vowed I would never again be honest with a council about my physical or emotional condition. The few times I have broken that vow since have not contradicted the basis for my vow.

The council's intransigence may have something to do with life in Montana. In these little towns, if you aren't working three jobs, if you are not constantly on the verge of physical, emotional, and marital collapse, you aren't working hard enough. Not many of the people here really do work that hard, but they all think they do, and many of them have the broken marriages to prove it. This may sound like bitterness. I suppose it is—I fight that too—but bitterness is easier to deal with than ambivalence. In bitterness I despise the church, and I want to leave. In ambivalence I cannot decide to leave the church and cannot decide to love the church.

Bitterness is bad, but ambivalence is worse. Ambivalence leads to pastoral disaster. Bitterness can drive us out of the ministry—not always a bad thing—but ambivalence paralyzes us, and that is *never* a good thing. Ambivalence is more likely to destroy a pastor's relationship with his or her family. That's because it is easier for a pastor's spouse to identify with bitterness than with ambivalence. One can unite around bitterness but not around ambivalence.

Bitterness is a burning cause, the center of the sun; ambivalence is cold space, formless and void. People who are bitter together can still love each other, people who are ambivalent together can't. My guess is that fewer bitter pastors become sexually involved with parishioners than do ambivalent pastors. A bitter pastor is usually mad at the whole blasted church. An ambivalent pastor isn't mad at anyone— on the outside—but he may be desperate for anyone's attention that will solve the loveless, indecisive state of his existence. Every church has people who thrive on solving the ambivalence issue for pastors. (Worse, the layperson who seems most sympathetic to your dilemma may be simply worming her way into your favor; she may be storing ammunition for a future battle.)

Of course, the struggle to avoid bitterness and ambivalence is common to all people. "That's just the way life is," semi-sympathetic laypeople will quickly point out. We live in a sinful world, and the church is infected with sin, as are its pastors. Church conflict and pastoral bruising are part of the deal. We never had the right to expect pastoral work to be conflict free. We never had the right to expect that conflict could be solved by common sense and love.

We can resign ourselves to the fact that our parishioners struggle with ambivalences too, and therefore we should simply accept it. But this doesn't work for us. Everyone else we know can conceivably pursue a vocation without love.

Sure, it's better if teachers, doctors, and artists love the people they work with. But they can perform their work without love and they can even do it well. The bind we face is that we can't do pastoral ministry without love. It isn't a series of tasks we do *with* love—rather, pastoral ministry *is* love, which we apply with a series of tasks. Preaching, teaching, calling, praying, even church administration are nothing but the consistent application of God's love to the church. God's love is the oil that the lampstand burns to produce the light of the world, and we are the bearers of that love.

To overcome the ambivalence that paralyzes our love, we must discover and embrace genuine love that can endure the battles and can motivate us to ministry. My guess is that the kind of love so subject to ambivalence is not a pure form of love in the first place. Maybe we need ball-cap-crisis heat to destroy the weak strains of childish love mixed in with our godly love. It is by no means beyond the ken of human nature to syncretize God's love poured into us by the Holy Spirit with the bratty love of our "inner child"—whatever that is. The ball-cap crisis wounded my inner child.

In pastoral ministry, we need plenty of childlike

faith, and we can't get enough childlike innocence, but to overcome ambivalence we must make the choice to love like Jesus. To solve the dilemma of ambivalence in pastoral ministry, we need a short course on the need for love in pastoral ministry, because ambivalence lies to us, leading us to believe we can do our work without love.

We also must define clearly the kinds of love pastors need—there's more than one. Ambivalence makes pastoral love seem impossible by meshing the different loves together into an indefinable, amorphous, massive demand for something like heroism. And when we're hurting badly, heroism is precisely what we can't manage. But then again, the drive to be a hero may be what gets us in these fixes. Heroism is not a form of pastoral love. Ambivalence has much less power over us if we know precisely what we need to do and then simply do it.

For example, the first love I discuss is *hesed*, a Hebrew word defined as "covenant love" or the "ability to bond." When I get flustered with my church and want to quit in a flurry of what I believe is holy anger (which is often nothing more than hurt feelings), I remind myself of my call to keep covenant with my church, and that means to keep my résumé where it belongs—in the drawer. I may not feel love when I'm mad, but I can keep my promises when I'm mad. Keeping covenant doesn't always feel like love, but it is a primary form of pastoral love.

Downright physical

But do we really need to love our church? Can't we do it another way?

Not according to Jesus. Jesus expressed the deep longing of the pastoral heart when he told his disciples:

> Abide in me as I abide in you. Just as the branch cannot bear fruit by itself unless it abides in the vine, neither can you unless you abide in me. I am the vine, you are the branches. Those who abide in me and I in them bear much fruit, because apart from me you can do nothing. (John 15:4–5)

These are the two facets of the pastoral heart: the spiritual desire to be with Christ and the material desire to do the work of leading others to follow him. For the pastor the two drives cannot be separated. They are united in our heart; we want to be with Christ and we want to lead others to him. They are united in our practice; we spend time with Christ and we spend time with the people we are called to serve. They are united in our effectiveness; the time we spend with Christ nourishes us and directs us to our work with people, and our work with people casts us back into the arms of Christ, for nourishment, direction, and rest.

Yet something remains unsatisfying about this dichotomy. Abiding in Christ and bearing fruit look like the two sides of our average day: prayer and Scripture-reading side by side with people-time.

But we require a more integrated view of this vital relationship. After all, the branch doesn't spend from eight till noon stuck in the vine sucking sap and from noon to five wandering around the vineyard looking for some grapes to ripen. The vine/branch relationship is fixed. The branch springs from the vine, is nourished by the vine, and at all times is supported by the vine. Fruit-bearing is rhythmic—the branch bears fruit at intervals. Nourishment and fruit-bearing is one act of abiding in Christ.

What does it mean to abide in Christ, anyway? In John 15 Jesus goes on to say:

> As the Father has loved me, so I have loved you; abide in my love. If you keep my commandments, you will abide in my love, just as I have kept my Father's commandments and abide in his love. I have said these things to you so that my joy may be in you, and that your joy may be complete. This is my commandment, that you love one another as I have loved you. No one has greater love than this, to lay down one's life for one's friends. (John 15:9–14)

"Abide in my love. . . ." To abide in Christ means to abide in his love. That makes it more clear.

"If you keep my commandments, you will abide in my love. . . ." The way to abide in Christ's love is by obeying his commandments. That makes abiding in Christ more concrete.

"This is my commandment, that you love one another as I have loved you. . . ." His specific commandment is that we love one another. This makes abiding in Christ concrete, practical, even attainable. Abiding in Christ is not vaguely mystical; it is starkly physical. We abide in Christ by loving one another in the fellowship of believers.

Jesus defines what it means to love one another when he says, "No one has greater love than this, to lay down one's life for one's friends." Abiding in Christ is physical in the same way that the relationship between the vine and the branch is physical. Furthermore, the relationship of the branch, the vine, and the fruit illuminates what it means to lay down one's life for one's friends: There may come a time for us to die to save a friend.

But that can only be done once. It is difficult to imagine how that view of laying down one's life can be construed as a long-term relationship of nourishment and fruit-bearing.

A superior understanding is that the vine lays down its life by providing the branch with its life reserves, and the branch lays down its life by providing the fruit with its life reserves gained from the vine. This describes the pastor's life. It is one in which we lay down our lives for our friends over a long period of time. This is our spiritual and material life with Christ.

In this union we bear fruit in a direct and positive way: "By this everyone will know that you are my disciples, if you have love for one another" (John 13:35). Yet by the way we do ministry much of the time, you'd think Jesus had said, "By this everyone will know you are my disciples, if you run great programs." Sadly, instead of knowing us by our love, the world knows us by our programs. The world doesn't care about our programs. They are as good at running programs as we are.

More than anything, our parishioners want us to

love them. More than anything, they want to love one
another. More than anything, the world longs for a
church of Christians that loves one another. We need
not worry about offending the world with our dogma,
our morality, or our worship. However, if we offend
the world by our fighting and lovelessness, we can expect nothing better than, "Whoever does not abide in
me is thrown away like a branch and withers; such
branches are gathered, thrown into the fire, and
burned" (John 15:6).

Some painful experiences in pastoral ministry
make us want to be religious hacks who hawk religion. We may become experts at manipulating human
behavior instead of simply behaving like humans.
Ambivalence girdles our nourishment from the vine.
We dry out. We become tinder.

Rather, ours is a ministry of love. There is no
other way for us to do our work. We can be religious
professionals without love. We can teach religion
without love. We can be religious hacks without love.
But there is no pastoral ministry without love.

Beachhead of love

However, we cannot under any circumstances
simply choose love. The burden of love is ultimately
unbearable. A person can choose to splay himself
spread eagle on a hand grenade in a foxhole *once*. No
one can choose to do that every day. The pastor
cannot choose love every day, the pastor can only
choose to yield his or her life to Christ every day. In

Christ the burden of love is not unbearable, for he tells us:

> Come to me, all you that are weary and are carrying heavy burdens, and I will give you rest. Take my yoke upon you, and learn from me; for I am gentle and humble in heart, and you will find rest for your souls. For my yoke is easy, and my burden is light. (Matt. 11:28–30)

This is why he tells us first to abide in him and then to love one another. The choice we make is to abide in Christ. Or perhaps better, it is Christ's choice that we abide in him. We know that we can love only after he has loved us first. Likewise, we can choose him only after he has chosen us. As Jesus goes on to say in John 15, "You did not choose me but I chose you. And I appointed you to go and bear fruit, fruit that will last . . ." (v. 16).

Jesus is being polite. Not only must he choose us, he must conquer us.

When Christ wants to love a congregation, he establishes his beachhead in the heart of the pastor. However, the heart of the ambivalent pastor is guarded, militarized territory. Land mines everywhere. Barbed, electrified wire abounds. Searchlights blast the beach. Jesus of Nazareth, our crucified and risen Lord, walks into the danger and absorbs the angry, brutal defense of our ambivalent heart. He uses no weapons of warfare, but he has ways of breaking our hearts wide open.

Often Jesus comes to me in the lives of people

who love me and whom I love. To use an extreme but unfortunate example, how many times has my dear family stepped forward to love me, trying to break through my weakness and depression, only to become entangled and shocked in the barbed wire around my heart. I didn't set it up for them. I thought I was setting it up for that lousy church! I forgot to take it all down before I walked in the door!

Does this break my heart? If it does not, I am a monster.

Thanks be to God, my heart is still capable of being broken. When I take ministry home with me, snapping at my wife and children, healing involves more than simply deciding to love my family more. That is not particularly difficult for me. I've got lots of experience apologizing, and they are well-experienced at forgiveness. Besides, I want desperately to love my family, and I enjoy doing it immensely.

My church? I wouldn't go so far as to say I want desperately to love my church. Sometimes I don't care at all, and it doesn't bother me not to care. Full healing for me, and for my family, requires me not simply to love them better; I must love my church better. I can accomplish that onerous task only by yielding to Christ's advances against my stubbornly ambivalent heart. He must be Lord. Jesus is the most stubborn warrior in the world, and he is the least compromising; he will cease and desist only upon unconditional surrender.

And he knows when I'm faking it with precious god-talk.

Jesus has been at war with me and I with him for

eighteen years. But at least when we are at war, I am not ambivalent! That is his way of keeping me in union with him, for when we are at war, we are still in love and still in union. When I stop caring, I am in trouble. He tells me, "I know your works; you are neither cold nor hot. I wish that you were either cold or hot. So, because you are lukewarm, and neither cold nor hot, I am about to spit you out of my mouth" (Rev. 3:15–16). Apparently, Jesus would rather I throw a rock at him than turn my back on him, as the astoundingly large number of psalms of lament seems to indicate.

In the next four chapters, I will discuss the different kinds of love Christ has given us to love our churches: what these loves are, why our churches need each type of love, and what happens when we fail to express them. Specifically, I will discuss why we must bond with our church, why we must show compassion to our church, why we must like our church (yes! why we must like it!), and how that all adds up to the *agape* sacrifice we make to Christ for his church.

3

TO BOND OR TO BAIL

HESED IS MY FAVORITE WORD in the Bible. I prefer it over every Hebrew or Greek word in the Scriptures. *Hesed* isn't more important or more inspired than other words. I just like the word. I like the way it sounds, and I like what it means.

I like the sound of *hesed*. The opening consonant is like the English "h," with its smoothness enhanced by a delicate guttural. Unlike like some gutturals that sound as if you're hacking up phlegm, *hesed*'s guttural is more like the sound of distant, rushing water. To pronounce *hesed*, the tongue constricts a little to the back of the throat, adding some friction to the airy "h" sound. The sound moves forward over the tip of the tongue, which arches up just behind the teeth to form the "s" sound, stopping briefly as the tongue quickly touches the top of the mouth to create the "d." The word proceeds easily with a nice rhythm.

They say that colors are hot or cold; words can be hot or cold too: *Hesed* is a cool word. It sounds refreshing, and it is about the ever-refreshing loving-kindness of God.

Hesed has many uses within the constellation of Hebrew words for love. You might call it a "flexi-lexi word." Some of its meanings are straightforward. *Hesed* can mean "love, kindness, mercy, and loyalty." However, just like the beginning consonant of *hesed* is an "h" sound augmented with a guttural, *hesed* is a word for love augmented with the meaning "keeping covenant."

This adds some friction to *hesed*'s basic meaning. *Hesed* means love, but it is the kind of love we show when we keep a promise or remain loyal to a friend. It isn't about promise-keeping in a legal or shrill way: "I'll keep my promise but I'm going to scratch my fingernails against this chalkboard the whole time." *Hesed* is about keeping our promises as a form of love, even if, perhaps, the party we are keeping covenant with has violated the letter or the spirit of the relationship. In that sense, to show *hesed* is to show grace.

The idea that *hesed* expresses grace caused the translators of the *King James Version* to translate *hesed* with words like "mercy" and "kindness," and with the most beautiful neo-logism in the history of the English language, "lovingkindness." No word in the English language could express more deeply what David had in mind when he prayed, "Because thy loving-kindness (*hesed*) is better than life, my lips shall praise thee" (Ps. 63:3, KJV).

The translators of the *New International Version* normally translate the word *hesed* with the English word *love* That's accurate enough, but doing so bleeds off the word's subtlety. It's a little like pronouncing the word *hesed* without the guttural.

Mercy, kindness, and lovingkindness communicate the upshot of *hesed*, but they don't really pin down its meaning. The translators of the *Revised Standard Version* and the *New Revised Standard Version* have given us the wonderful phrase *steadfast love* to express *hesed* as "promise-keeping love."

After Moses made two new tablets of stone, as he hid in the cleft of the rock, "The Lord passed before him, and proclaimed, 'The Lord, the Lord, a God merciful and gracious, slow to anger, and abounding in steadfast love and faithfulness'" (Ex. 34:6).

The steadfast love of the Lord preserves our lives: "When I thought, 'My foot is slipping,' your steadfast love, O Lord, held me up" (Ps. 94:18). "Have mercy on me, O God, according to your steadfast love; according to your abundant mercy blot out my transgressions" (Ps. 51:1).

Steadfast love is the long, stubborn love of God. In *hesed* God stays faithful to us long after we have forfeited our right to remain in covenant with him. The New Covenant is in the Old Covenant in God's *hesed*. That God sent his Son to die for us is his loving sacrifice for us, but that sacrifice springs from his steadfast love. God did not take pleasure in sacrificing his Son. Rather, God takes pleasure in bonding himself to a people and doing whatever it takes to save them and keep them in his love. God loves us so much in his steadfast love that he sent his Son to die for our sins.

God loves bonding himself to a people, and he

loves knowing that his steadfast love makes his people feel secure in their relationship to him. This is the kind of love God showed Abraham. It is the kind of love God showed the Israelites in redeeming them out of slavery in Egypt. It is the kind of love God shows us when Paul declares, "For I am convinced that neither death, nor life, nor angels, nor rulers, nor things present, nor things to come, nor powers, nor height, nor depth, nor anything else in all creation, will be able to separate us from the love of God in Christ Jesus our Lord" (Rom. 8:38–39).

Hesed is love that will not separate. It is the love Ruth showed Naomi. God's love may discipline us; it may withdraw from us for a while to test our faithfulness, but we are never beyond the reach of God's *hesed*. Whatever else is involved in the endless debate of whether or not we can lose our salvation, our arguments are infinitely poorer by not figuring God's *hesed* into the equation. The New Testament, in which God's steadfast love is fulfilled, possesses no word that communicates the content of *hesed*, presumably because Greek has no such word.

Or perhaps the New Testament doesn't possess such a word because its meaning is captured and completed in the Word made flesh, in the life, death, and resurrection of Jesus Christ, our great Shepherd. To be shepherds like our great Shepherd, our lives must embody, as his did, the *hesed* of God.

Hesed in action

Moses is Scripture's archetype of a servant of God showing *hesed* to the people of God. Moses' example is helpful because the Scriptures provide us with a detailed look at his long ministry. Showing *hesed* to the people of God was the burden of his life, and it was, ultimately, the victory of his life. Nevertheless, Moses' flesh cried out under the yoke of demonstrating the *hesed* of God.

Moses was raised for something better than baby-sitting 400,000 whiners. His Egyptian upbringing taught him leadership, and I cannot help but think that Moses was well acquainted with the benefits and respect that normally accompany positions of worldly power.

During his exile, tending sheep in the wilderness, Moses' benefits were meager; so were his responsibilities. But the encounter at the burning bush changed that forever. From that point on, he had the responsibilities of a Pharaoh with the salary package of a bag lady.

Moses became the instrument of God's saving love. That sounds wonderful in theory, but it isn't all that great in practice, because generally speaking, God's people don't want to be saved; they want to be fixed. They don't want to be led, they want to be managed. The Israelites wanted Moses to fix the problem of slavery. They didn't want to cross the Red Sea and travel to Canaan. They didn't mind Jethro's suggestion that Moses divide up the leadership responsibilities. What they didn't want to do was cross the Jordan to fight the Canaanites.

As is well known, the people of God fought against Moses constantly. They threatened to stone him a couple of times, but that would have seemed a mercy to him compared with the burden of their constant grumbling. When he was at his best, Moses didn't take it personally, he just told them, "Your complaining is not against us but against the Lord" (Ex. 16:8).

But often his burden was too much to bear. At one point he prayed to God:

> Why have you treated your servant so badly? Why have I not found favor in your sight, that you lay the burden of all this people on me? Did I conceive all this people? Did I give birth to them, that you should say to me, "Carry them in your bosom, as a nurse carries a sucking child," to the land that you promised on oath to their ancestors? Where am I to get meat to give to all this people? For they come weeping to me and say, "Give us meat to eat!" I am not able to carry all this people alone, for they are too heavy for me. If this is the way you are going to treat me, put me to death at once—if I have found favor in your sight—and do not let me see my misery" (Num. 11:11–15).

Moses' most compelling and phenomenal execution of *hesed* was when he interceded with God to save the people who had made his life so utterly miserable after they had sweet-talked Aaron into making them a golden calf. In this instance of sheer pastoral love, Moses shows *hesed* for God's people by using God's *hesed* in his argument against God:

> The Lord said to Moses, "I have seen this

people, how stiff-necked they are. Now let me alone, so that my wrath may burn hot against them and I may consume them; and of you I will make a great nation."

But Moses implored the Lord his God, and said, "O Lord, why does your wrath burn hot against your people, whom you brought out of the land of Egypt with great power and with a mighty hand? Why should the Egyptians say, 'It was with evil intent that he brought them out to kill them in the mountains, and to consume them from the face of the earth'? Turn from your fierce wrath; change your mind and do not bring disaster on your people. Remember Abraham, Isaac, and Israel, your servants, how you swore to them by your own self, saying to them, 'I will multiply your descendants like the stars of heaven, and all this land that I have promised I will give to your descendants, and they shall inherit it forever.'" And the Lord changed his mind about the disaster that he planned to bring on his people. (Ex. 32:9–14)

Of all the types of love that God demonstrates and that we emulate, *hesed* is probably the one love we can consistently, and boldly, use in our arguments against God as we intercede for our people. Praying to God's *hesed* prays directly to the heart of God's nature. God tells us, "I will be gracious (*hanan*) to whom I will be gracious, and will show mercy (*racham*) on whom I will show mercy" (Ex. 33:19). *Hesed* appeals not only to God's promise to show love to a people, it appeals to God's love of keeping covenant. But the prayer must come from the heart of the pastor's nature, as an expression of the Spirit's prayer within. Though Moses spoke his prayer rather nicely, often our prayers for God's mercy upon the very people who give us so much trouble are the Spirit's prayers from within us that are, quite frankly, "sighs too deep for words" (Rom. 8:26).

We know that Jesus intercedes for us and for the whole church at the right hand of God (Rom. 8:34). Perhaps some of his intercession moves directly through us, for we know that "God has sent the Spirit of his Son into our hearts, crying, 'Abba! Father!'" (Gal. 4:6).

Moses showed the people of God the *hesed* of God by interceding for them. The result of his intercession was that he stayed with his call. The Israelites knew the *hesed* of God concretely in the *hesed* of Moses.

This display of *hesed* is the pastor's call too. It stands as a truth of pastoral ministry that we are called upon to show the people we serve *hesed*, the steadfast love of God.

We do this by staying with our job. But in a deeper sense, we do it by uniting with a congregation spiritually and emotionally in and with the steadfast love God has for them. Moses was called upon to bind himself to the Israelites because God had bound himself to them. Moses' bond to Israel was fixed in God's bond to Israel.

When we enter a pastoral relationship with a congregation, whatever else is involved in the contract, we bind ourselves to that congregation in and with the bond that God has with them. Perhaps the greatest spiritual issue between a pastor and a congregation is whether a bond is formed between them or not; that is, whether they can show one another *hesed.*

We don't have to like the bond. I wonder if when in our frustration we say we dislike our congregation, what we are really saying is that we dislike the bond we have with them, or more particularly, the covenant bond God has called us to. When we think we are grumbling about our church, maybe we are grumbling against God.

The bond

When a church and a pastor do not bond, the church cannot grow—in numbers, in commitment to one another and to God, to mission, to worship, and to a deeper spirituality. The simple reason is that all growth involves change and risk, which causes most individuals and all congregations profound anxiety and threatens to keep us from taking the steps to growth.

Without question, every step into the risk that change entails involves faith, but we exercise all faith—even the blindest steps of faith—in a God who is faithful to his promises, who in fact loves to keep his promises, and who loves to show his love precisely in keeping his promises after we have broken our promises to him.

But if God's servants continually break their promises, this tacitly impugns God's integrity. Pastors do not have to be perfect in keeping their promises; Moses was certainly not perfect, and neither was another great example of *hesed*, David. But we do need to keep the basic bond of our promise—and that is to stick with our job until we are done.

The Lord who is our Shepherd leads us beside still waters. He is present with us as we pass through the valley of the shadow of death. But maybe pastors are his rod and his staff, living instruments of his *hesed*. If we cannot be instruments of God's *hesed* to our congregations, if we cannot bond with them, then our people will have a distorted view of God's steadfast love to the point of doubting it completely.

I shall not forget my first meeting with a high school youth group I was called to work with. I sat next to a girl as the group was gathering—she was obviously one of the leaders of the group—and I started a conversation with her. She ignored my inquiries and simply said to me, "I'm waiting for you to quit like all the rest."

I decided I needed to see the group through the pain of losing so many leaders.

Sure I had to do good work, but more than anything, I had to stay. I had to show them that someone loved them enough to stay with them. In this case, the time wasn't long. I worked with that youth group three-and-a-half years before I was called to Montana to serve two country churches.

But my three-and-a-half years there was 300 percent longer than previous ministries, and it was enough. The church has had an effective youth ministry ever since. That it does is due to the church's commitment to ministry. But for that commitment to have a chance, someone had to break through the group's cycle of failure.

My two new churches in Montana were ninety-nine and ninety-seven years old. I studied the little histories they produced as they prepared for their 100-year anniversaries. The history of the pastorates in both churches reads like grocery-store gossip rags. The pastorates normed at two and three years. The two churches shared a fine pastor in the 1950s. His ministry lasted eight years, and he and his wife were remembered with great fondness. After he left, however, the cycle returned.

By the time I reached the churches, the parishioners felt a great deal of ambivalence toward pastors. They had been burned so many times they couldn't embrace a pastor. Early on a local smart-alec confronted me in front of the bank: "Preacher, you won't last here; you'll be gone soon like all the rest."

He and his wife went to another church in town. They'd left ours years before during one of its tough times. I answered him quick as a whip, "Jack, you'll be dead and gone before I leave this church."

By the time I left, he wasn't dead, but he and his wife had moved out of town. Neither church has any idea how many times during that nine-and-a-half years that I wanted to quit; I wonder if the reason I didn't quit was because of Jack's comment.

The ministry in both churches went along fine until the fifth year. Then things began to slowly unravel. Some people said my sermons were boring. Even some close friends began questioning how I spent my time. I felt the people begin to distance themselves from me. The church peppered my leadership initiatives with pseudo-tough questions, with reticence that bordered on annoyance. I began to hear things like: "People are saying this and that about such and such." The *people*, I have since learned, were phantoms with less substance than an Elvis sighting.

I compared my situation with other pastors I'd known who'd struggled with churches with histories like mine. Most had bailed. Others stuck it out and broke through to good times. I began to think about my church's "leadership envelope," which is roughly the age of the church divided by the number of its pastors. If the average tenure is three years or less— and the previous twenty years have not contradicted the cycle—that portends trouble. By staying four years, and showing no signs of leaving, I caused the church dissonance, something like the turbulence a jet hits just before it breaks the sound barrier.

The churches experienced dissonance on at least two fronts. First, the churches may have wanted to ditch me before I ditched them. Conventional wisdom suggests those dumped out of too many romances defend themselves by making sure they become the dump-er instead of the dumpee. As soon as a relationship becomes dicey, they begin to look at their tattered list of fifty ways to leave their lover. As I thought through the history of the churches, my compassion grew. Except for the one pastor in the '50s, the churches had no reason to doubt that bad pastors have to be edged out, and good pastors leave.

A curious phenomenon clinched this insight for

me. Even the people who began questioning my time and my sermons and my calling and my leadership judgment found ways to let my wife and I know how devastated they would be if we left!

Second, the two undeniable, historical facts for both churches were (1) they had survived for one hundred years, and (2) their survival was not due to stable pastoral leadership. Both of these churches knew how to survive without a pastor, and they were proud of it: "Pastors come and go, but we hold the church together." They had every right to feel this way. But I was staying longer than they were accustomed to.

They were good people, devout, tough Christians. Most liked me and respected me, but corporately they didn't know how to deal with a pastor staying longer than three years. Would my tenure threaten the existence of the church? They trusted me to preach and call, and do weddings and funerals, but could they trust me to exercise leadership?

Since I had more stubbornness than good sense, and the churches had more good sense than stubbornness, it all worked out. The older members in both churches saved the day. Though the churches had bonded with only one pastor in 100 years, that was enough. They eventually defaulted in their feelings back thirty years to the pastor in the fifties and realized I was like him, and not like the ones since. That church memory led us through to victory, along with a whole lot of prayer (and the fact that I remained determined to outlast Jack).

One result of my long stay surprised me: I discovered that many parishioners with deep, humble faiths were insecure in their standing with God. During my nine years in these churches, I heard more questions about that subject than in any church I'd served. I have my own theological views on these matters, and I have pastoral strategies to help people. But not much seemed to help. As I look back, with one exception, by the time I left, most of their questions seemed to have answered themselves. I don't think much of it was due to my preaching or teaching. I believe a lot of their personal anguish got solved just because I showed them the *hesed* of God by staying.

Both churches accomplished a lot during my tenure. But what I am most proud of—because it was the hardest and the most important thing I did—was that I stayed.

4

COMPASSION FROM THE GUT

I WAS A YOUNG PASTOR in my first parish, and a family in the church was nursing a dying grandmother. I did not visit the family. I wasn't lazy, I was scared. I didn't know what to do. I didn't know that doing something was the very thing I shouldn't do, and all I needed to do was be there.

When the lady died, I was so embarrassed that I never visited the family or even called them on the phone. I was not asked to do the funeral. Over the years the family never mentioned it, and as far as I could tell, they never held it against me. They knew I was a young buck without a brain in my head.

I can see now why I failed, but I can't forget the failure. Thankfully. When I want to ignore a hospital call, I remember that circumstance or ones like it— and I get up and make the call.

I'll admit it: a lot of times I make calls on the sick because doing so is my job, not because I feel compassion for them. Visiting someone in traction just to keep my proverbial hind end out of the sling isn't the high standard I'm reaching for in ministry, but it keeps me out of trouble.

I don't quake at the thought of a parishioner scolding me for missing his or her stay in the hospital. Apologizing is never pleasant, but most people are quite forgiving. The real trouble I get into when I don't visit the sick is with my guilty conscience. It is more difficult to assuage than an angry parishioner. My parishioners forgive and forget, but my conscience does not suffer from Alzheimer's!

Visiting the suffering to satisfy the conscience is low-level pastoral work. As a form of following Jesus, it beats disobedience, but it never escapes tepidity, which left to itself cools to bloodless apathy.

Granted that it is pathetic to make whipped-dog pastoral visits, should I make these calls with this motivation?

My parishioners assume I arrive out of love. Should I be honest enough to announce that I have come in order to avoid the discomfort of a guilty conscience? I can't do that. The person might get sicker. And it would short-cut God's ability to use my bleak obedience. My conscience is relentless, but it is also smart; it forces me to call, not because a lukewarm attempt at pastoral work is better than nothing, but because it knows that God creates out of nothing. I call by faith, not by feeling.

When I arrive in the room of suffering, love takes over. My heart beats faster, my consciousness sharpens, and my innards feel less stable. Compassion happens. What began onerously ends sympathetically.

Human kindness ignited by a Spirit spark leads to a Spirit prayer for healing. What a strange turn of events! I walk into a hospital room grumpy because I'm missing the fourth quarter of a football game, and I walk out feeling like Mother Teresa, Jr. It rarely fails.

Is this hypocritical?

If it is hypocritical, it is only so to the extent that being human makes us all look like hypocrites at times. It is deeply human to respond compassionately to suffering. It is also characteristically human to feel less compassion from a distance than in person. This even seems to have been the case with Jesus. There are numerous examples in the Gospels where Jesus was moved to compassion for someone when he encountered them in person. One time a leper came to Jesus, "begging him, and kneeling he said to him, 'If you choose, you can make me clean.' Moved with pity, Jesus stretched out his hand and touched him, and said to him, 'I do choose. Be made clean!'" (Mark 1:40–41).

The human life of the Son of God gave him sympathy for our struggles against temptation. "For we do not have a high priest who is unable to sympathize with our weaknesses, but we have one who in every respect has been tested as we are, yet without sin" (Heb. 4:15). The steadfast love of God produced the Incarnation. One result of the Incarnation was the immediate, physical experience of the human suffering of Jesus, and that produced compassion. Compassion takes flesh; the main words for compassion in both Testaments are words that have to do with flesh.

Splaxna: *shaky guts*

The big word for compassion in the New Testament is *splaxna*, a Greek word from which we get the English word "spleen." In Greek literature *splaxna* is used at various times for almost all the vital organs, but basically it means something like "guts." Splaxna is the shakiness we feel in our guts when moved by contact with suffering.

Compassion is the love that most fully exploits the union of body and soul. *Splaxna* occurs in our soul and in our body. Compassion happens as our disturbed soul pours its love-shock into the body. Compassion is experienced simultaneously as we feel this kind of love in our body and in our soul at the same time. The experience of compassion is deeply spiritual in its genesis and profoundly physical in its revelation. Even in Jesus.

When Lazarus died, Jesus stayed away from the family for two days. Then he led his fearful disciples back to Bethany by the scruff of their necks. When Martha heard that Jesus was coming, she ran out to meet him. She scolded him and begged him, "Lord, if you had been here, my brother would not have died. But even now I know that God will give you whatever you ask of him" (John 11:21–22).

Jesus responded to her theologically: "Your brother will rise again."

Martha answered him theologically: "I know that he will rise again in the resurrection on the last day."

Jesus continued, "I am the resurrection and the life. Those who believe in me, even though they die, will live, and everyone who lives and believes in me will never die. Do you believe this?"

Martha said to him, "Yes, Lord, I believe that you are the Messiah, the Son of God, the one coming into the world" (John 11:23–27). Satisfied, Martha ran to Mary to tell her Jesus had come.

When Mary heard Jesus had come, she ran to him and fell at his feet, weeping, and said to him, "Lord, if you had been here, my brother would not have died" (John 11:32).

Jesus responded to her differently: "When Jesus saw her weeping, and the Jews who came with her also weeping, he was greatly disturbed in spirit and deeply moved" (John 11:33). He responded to Martha's theological confrontation with loving theology. He responded to Mary's tearful confrontation with weeping love issuing from a disturbed spirit and "shaky guts."

Compassion is Incarnation love: "The Word became flesh and blood, and moved into the neighborhood" (John 1:14, The Message). Compassion is the physical movement into the presence of suffering and the spiritual movement into the void created by the sense of abandonment that suffering brings.

Racham: *womb love*

In the Old Testament, the big word used for God's compassion is *racham*, which also means "womb." God's compassion for us is like the compassion a mother has for the child in her womb. The ideal is Mary, who compassionately, faithfully held the compassion of God incarnate in her womb.

The coherence of divine love, parental love, and pastoral love is perhaps more pronounced in compassion than in all other types of love. The identity among the three is present in the traditional designation of the pastor/priest as "Father." The apostle Paul likened his pastoral work to nursing: "We were gentle among you, like a nurse tenderly caring for her own children" (1 Thess. 2:7).

Again, God is the model: "As a father has compassion (*racham*) for his children, so the Lord has compassion (*racham*) for those who fear him. For he knows how we were made; he remembers that we are dust" (Ps. 103:13–14).

God has compassion on our vulnerable lives. Parents have compassion for their ever so vulnerable children. And pastors must have compassion for the vulnerable lives of the people they serve. When I walk into the room of suffering, so often eyes look up at me with a deep helplessness that say:

- "How could I have gotten into this mess?"
- "I am lost."
- "I can't go on."
- "Can you help me?"

I also see these eyes at weddings. She came down the aisle dressed like Barbie, except the wedding dress had a maternity cut. She was sixteen, he was eighteen, and they were nice kids. As the father of teenage daughters, I knew the ceremony would be difficult for me emotionally. I didn't want to bust up, so before the service, I told myself that this kind of thing had been happening for thousands of years. It wasn't difficult to recall several couples in the church, in their fifties now, who'd started the same way. Funny thing was, they had some of the best marriages in the church.

Having sufficiently objectivized the situation, I headed to the sanctuary with reasonable confidence I could make it through the service. Everything would have been fine except that my last thought as I entered the sanctuary was, *Do this service the way you would want it done for one of your daughters.*

As she came down the aisle with her dad, I scanned the participants. The groom beamed. The bride glowed. Her dad winced. Her mom cried. His parents bawled. The maid of honor shook, and the best man looked like he was in another world. My voice box began to constrict, and my abdominal muscles weren't holding me up too well.

After the processional, just before the main part of the service, as the bride and the groom stood in front of me, silent, I waited just a second to look into their utterly vulnerable, melted eyes.

This is the point of decision for me: Do I carry on from here dispassionately like a justice of the peace, or do I enter the empty space of their humility and neediness, compassionately, in the name of the God and Father of us all? One is culturally relevant, the other is spiritually relevant. I decided to love them. I began the service as best I could, scratchy voice and all.

God was good to us. He gave me strength, together with love, and we worshiped and celebrated with tears and with joy, just as I would have wanted it had she been my own daughter or he my own son.

It is precisely vulnerability that is so difficult to deal with. It throws the tenuous nature of our existence into our face. Entering another's vulnerability, identifying with it, and allowing it to enter us and move us is the goal of compassion.

To say that happens naturally isn't to say that it comes easily. Even parents often enter their children's vulnerability out of duty. It is always worth it, but it is never easy. It shouldn't be easy. Every opportunity to show compassion to our family, our church, or to people on the street is a decision to enter pain.

My goal is not to drain compassion of passion, but to secure compassion as a permanent and reliable feature in our ministries through understanding the proper role of duty in compassion. Compassion is serendipitous, but it is not haphazard. Compassion requires the willingness to put ourselves in proximity to suffering and the willingness to feel it once we are there. Often the willingness is sheer choice. Relegating compassion to a rational decision may seem heartless, but it keeps us working at something that is very difficult.

Bringing God or playing God?

What does compassion do for people? It heals.

Jesus showed compassion to the people he healed, and it was more than simply a nice gesture; his compassion was part of his cure. Compassion and prayer both have healing power. Twenty years ago the medical community discovered that simple human compassion shown by hospital personnel helped people get better faster. All of a sudden, nurses got nicer. In recent years they discovered that prayer helps people get better too. Now even secular hospitals employ chaplains. People can be healed by compassion without prayer, and people can be healed by prayer without compassion. An atheist's compassion may have healing power, paradoxically, like the prayers of a loveless pastor.

But when you combine compassion and prayer, one and one equals three. This is well known. What fascinates me most about compassion is that, in my observation, compassion has the power to solve or at least alleviate the intellectual problem of evil.

Talking broken people through the problem of evil is about as satisfying as talking humble people through their agony about whether they are saved. Theological insights and Bible verses help a little but not a lot. The only sufficient answers to "Job" questions come from God—personally. The sincere Christian with grave doubts about his or her salvation needs the assurance of God's love directly from God. The broken soul who doubts the existence of good in her world of personal horror needs the same kind of assurance—directly from God.

How do pastors bring God's love to people? We pray for them, and we bring God's compassion to them. Sometimes God's compassion can take the form of theological dialogue.

A woman in her early thirties who had attended worship several Sundays in a row stayed around after

75

the service. She walked up to me and asked in a desperate tone, "Can we talk . . . right now?"

"Sure, I guess so."

We sat in a pew, and she began to tremble, but she came to the point: "I usually don't come to church. I have a hard time with God." She paused to catch her breath and to test her resolve. She turned her eyes to the ground to say what she had to say, but she did not speak timidly.

"My father and my uncle molested me all through my childhood until I moved out and joined the army. How could God allow that?"

She said it that quickly and that bluntly. At which point she crumpled and began to cry.

She swore and said, "I knew I'd do this."

"Don't worry about it," I said. "I listen to people cry for a living."

I was glad when she snickered. I could tell she was working hard to regain her composure, so I waited until she could look up again. She looked up at me, surprised, I think, that I didn't scold her for cussing. She waited for my answer. She really thought I might have an answer to her question.

I gave her the only answer I know: "I don't know."

"What do you mean, 'you don't know?'" she retorted with an edge of anger.

I think she felt cheated, as if her profound candor deserved a deep answer. Which it did. I could only respond to her with candor.

"I know it doesn't sound like much of an answer," I said, "but the reason I say that I don't know why things like that happen is that I really don't know. I don't why God does what he does, or why he allows what he allows, or why bad things happen at all. God doesn't tell me. I really don't know."

This seemed to calm her down.

Theological honesty is a form of compassion with power to soothe. As I spoke to her, I thought about how much I really do believe in God's providence in our lives. But just because I believe God is sovereign doesn't mean I have the slightest idea why things happen, or how or why he allows things to happen.

But to respond blithely that God didn't have anything to do with her situation, that somehow stuff like this just happens by chance or is caused by the devil and that God doesn't have any say in the matter at all, would have failed her grievously. It would have been tantamount to saying that God does not exist.

In pastoral care we have two choices: we can bring God to people, or we can play God with people. I have learned I don't need to answer people's questions so much as I need to bring the answer to them in the form of compassion. I allowed myself to feel her pain—as best I could and as overwhelming as doing so was for me—and maybe what I felt for her was some of God's pain for her. That's what she really needed to feel—God's pain for her suffering. The problem of evil is incomprehensible, but it is not insoluble; compassion dissolves it.

She and I talked longer about the trials of her childhood, and then I told her something that every person in her situation needs to hear: "I don't have a lot of answers for this kind of stuff, but I can tell you this—I believe you. I believe every word you've told me. And even though I've never experienced what you have experienced, and I can't begin to imagine what it must have been like to go through all that or what it must be like to live with it now, believe me, I believe you when you tell me how horrible it was then and how horrible it is now to try to live. It took a lot of guts for you to come here today and to be as honest with me as you have been. I know that God honors your honesty. And who knows, maybe, with time, love, and prayer, you can receive some healing for all this."

She expressed her appreciation for what I'd said, but she still needed to test my compassion. She needed to know whether the church was a place where she could get some help. She just blurted it out: "I can't say 'Our Father' when you pray the Lord's Prayer." She looked me dead in the eye as she said it. She was looking for a flinch. I didn't.

"That's okay. Don't say it. It's fine with me. I'm sure it's okay with God. He understands your problem with that."

I smiled a little when she said, "You mean God isn't going to strike me dead?"

"Nope. But maybe, someday, you will be able to pray 'Our Father.' Don't rush it. Don't feel guilty about it. Just watch. Freedom to call God 'Father' might just sneak up on you."

"That would be nice," she said.

We talked a bit longer, and she left. I was phys-

ically and spiritually annihilated the rest of the day.
She has hardly missed a Sunday in the last four years.

Compassion in gear

Why is compassion so difficult?

Because it's hard to enter doubt, chaos, and evil.
Yet that is what heals people. So we have to do it. But
we can only take so much.

She has her own life to live, her own traumatic
past to deal with, but she's not the only one in our
church with her problem or with problems of that
magnitude, and I know there's lots I don't know
about. Too much of this creates a spiritual and emotional overload, which pushes too many watts
through our tender circuits. For thirty-six hours after
I visited with that woman, I felt like my mental moth-
erboard had been struck by lightening.

Health care workers of all types deal with this
every day. Pastors meet it less often, but we suffer
from this kind of overload more than the others.
Why? Maybe the reason is that the people we care for
are family. Even this woman, little as I knew her, was
like a sister.

As pastors, we have numerous family members
who are sick, dying, in nursing homes, confused, de-
pressed, having marriage problems, abusing drugs
and alcohol, unsaved, falling away from Christ, fighting with someone else in the family, and on and on.
These people are not our clients. They are not our patients. They are our family. Competent doctors don't
treat their family members. And competent psychol-

ogists don't counsel their children, their spouse, their siblings, or their parents.

But we do this kind of thing all the time, and we *must* do it, because God does not have clients or patients. God has children. And God requires that we show his children his father-womb-gut-love compassion.

The pain and drain of compassion tempts us to make family into clients and to turn compassion into bedside manner. For the most part, our people know when we are doing this. So what? What happens to our people when we do not show them compassion in their suffering? Lukewarmness, bitterness, backsliding, and atheism can happen.

The intellectual problem of evil crushes the soul not so much because bad things happen to us but because of the festering wounds that have not been healed by compassion. I remember a philosophy professor in college who could not resist a chance to blast religion. Following one of his volleys at faith, a devout student asked him, with kindness, why he did not believe in God. He answered uncharacteristically gently: "Because I have seen too many starving kittens."

What an opportunity to show him compassion by simply listening to the stories behind that comment!

What kills faith is not so much that people go through the valley of the shadow of death; it is that during and after their suffering they never felt God's rod and staff comforting them. God is the great Shepherd, and we are his rod and his staff. When we don't shepherd people through their pain, they don't wonder where we are so much as they wonder where God is. Scripture tells us that God "heals the broken-hearted, and binds up their wounds" (Ps. 147:3). When we heal hearts and bind wounds, people experience God's healing. When we refuse to, they wonder why God says he heals but won't help them.

By consistently failing to show compassion, we symbolize an uncaring god of fate that our people cannot help but despise. That is when they begin to stumble over the problem of evil. When we fail to show compassion, we push people toward ungodliness.

So yes. My conscience is seared with the record of times I have failed to care for people. So often they forgive. But I have seen some of them leave the church family and fall away from the Lord. Is it all my fault? I know it isn't. People have choices to make. I know I am not the only person in the church called to share God's love. And sometimes I stay away from parishioners in pain because I know that God wants them to struggle toward his love. My job isn't to rush into every situation without discernment! I am not God; I am made of dust too. As was Jesus, who retired frequently to a mountain for rest and spiritual refreshment. Nevertheless, etched into my conscience is a record of casualties due to my failure to care.

So I make hospital calls, not because I necessarily feel a whole lot of love for the person but to keep my conscience out of trouble and my compassion in gear. God honors that. He wants me to have a clear conscience in my work. And he wants his children to know that they are loved.

5

HOW TO BEFRIEND A CHURCH

MR. JONES'S HUNCHED-OVER, ox-yoke shoulders framed a body once six-feet-three inches tall, but after ninety years gravity was winning. You couldn't have rendered a teaspoon of fat from his trim physique. His bull pine arms clung tightly to their shoulder sockets; years of bucking bales left them permanently angled at the elbows. His powerful hands could slam-dunk the earth.

His strength was intact, but his joints didn't cooperate. His hearing was shot; and he saw only shapes, no details. I never heard him sing, but when he spoke, his bass voice sounded like it originated from the center of the earth. A nurse cared for him full-time, including bringing him to church. The piety was hers alone.

In personality, Mr. Jones was as subtle as his frame.

The pretty white country church held about 120, but we felt blessed to gather forty-five on a Sunday.

We hoped for new families. Some visited, few stayed. To remain, you had to like Mr. Jones as much as we did because at any point in the service he might say just about anything—loudly. Ostensibly, he was speaking only to his nurse. But when he leaned over to whisper in her long-suffering ear, his God-given basso allowed everyone to hear every word. None of us will ever know if Mr. Jones couldn't manage discretion, or if he was just an old coot who figured he'd earned the right to be a public nuisance. I suspect the latter. But since he never upset us too much with his outbursts, he probably never accomplished his goal.

Once during my pastoral prayer he supplicated his nurse, "Who is that up there, anyway?" (Quoting him verbatim violates reasonable norms of language for Christian publishing!)

Commonly, about ten minutes into the sermon, he'd turn to his nurse and say, "Isn't he done yet?"

Mr. Jones was a church-growth nightmare. We loved him, but we never thought visitors did. Then again, when his bones aged past coming to church, our numbers didn't increase. It saddened me to see him go. It made preaching a little less tense, but it forced me to work harder at keeping people awake. When he died, his nurse returned to her home church.

I will always consider it an irony that an old man cussing during the Lord's Prayer didn't perturb people, but a couple of kids wearing ball caps blew the place to pieces.

Can I like this kind of a situation? Do I need to like it? Do pastors need to like the church they serve?

I didn't think I needed to like my church when I began pastoral ministry.

Philos: *the gutsy love*

The word *like* is like *nice*, and *nice* is a wimpy word. There are a lot of things about most churches that aren't nice. An old man bleating expletives during worship isn't nice.

In every one of the four rural churches I have served, certain people have enjoyed visiting with their friends in the pews before worship. For them it was an opportune time to fellowship with other Christians. I called them the Informalites. Each church also had certain people who liked *quiet* before worship. They didn't think talking to their friends before worship was the thing to do. I called them the Formalites. The Formalites thought the Informalites were rude. And the Informalites thought the Formalites were stuffy. Both groups liked accosting me with their definition of "nice" in opposition to the other group's definition. The Formalites and the Informalites each expected me to enforce their idea of niceness with pastoral police action. The Formalites wanted fifteen minutes of marshal law before service, and the Informalites wanted fifteen minutes of anarchy.

What I didn't like was being asked to be everyone's cop of niceness. (These debates resembled a Jackie Chan movie. And yes, I did all my own stunts.)

But I have become convinced that we must like our churches and its parishioners. I take this from the New Testament words *phileo* and *philos*, which can mean "to love," "to befriend," "to hug," and "to kiss."

Taken together, they imply "to like." We often give the *philos* words a short sheet in our New Testament studies because *agape* is exalted as divine love, and *philos* is relegated to human love. There is plenty of truth to this; after all, Jesus' sacrifice was an act of *agape*. We cannot pastor our congregations without *agape*. But historically speaking they crucified Jesus not because of who he loved but because of who he *liked*. The powers of his day might have endured a mission by Jesus of *agape* love to tax collectors and sinners. Christ's ministry was a mission of *agape*, but for him, *agape* meant befriending sinners. Liking sinners could not be tolerated. The Pharisees did not accuse Jesus of loving sinners; they accused him of befriending (*philos*) sinners.

For instance, when Jesus called Levi away from the tax collector's table, some of the Pharisees may have been impressed. But for Jesus to attend the party at Levi's house to celebrate the man's new life with his old friends was unacceptable.

If Jesus had preached the message of John the Baptist at the party, the Pharisees might have been impressed. But "eating and drinking with tax collectors and sinners" isn't preaching to them. Rather, Jesus shared fellowship with sinners. He must have even appeared to be enjoying the company of the people around him. "The Son of Man has come eating and drinking, and you say, 'Look, a glutton and a drunkard, a friend (*philos*) of tax collectors and sinners!'" (Luke 7:34). To a Pharisee, this kind of thing is definitely not nice.

Jesus didn't preach the message of John the Baptist; instead, he lived out John's baptism by identifying himself with sinners. He could not have ministered to them if he had not liked them, for to like someone is to reflect to them that they are made in the image of God. To like someone is to affirm in particular what it says in general in Genesis about all creation: "God saw everything that he had made, and indeed, it was very good" (Gen. 1:31). We stew over how to improve someone's self-image; Jesus simply befriended people, and in so doing affirmed they were made in God's image.

Most people have a hard time believing that God is with them if not a single human being who claims to know Jesus wants to spend time with them. We need someone to reflect our self-worth to us in person through positive, life-affirming friendship.

This is true for churches as well, especially the small churches that get passed from pastor to pastor. They eventually learn that it is easier to dump a pastor than it is to be dumped by one, and they become extremely difficult to like in the process. A pastor can preach to these churches that they are the body of Christ, but they will do everything in their power to convince him or her that they are *not* the body of Christ.

These churches need a pastor who will stick with them (bond with them), have sympathy for their dysfunctional existence (have true compassion for them), and even *like* them. Otherwise, they will never believe deep down in their fractured, complex, corporate soul that they truly are the body of the living Christ—so they can start acting that way.

Of course, all of this requires sacrifice (*agape*), which I will discuss in the next chapter. But merely making a sacrifice for a person or a church does not necessarily improve his or her self-image. Liking a person does. Liking a person or a church, finding the individuals pleasant, beautiful, and good, is the genesis of genuine, positive self-image.

Proverbs 8 is the song of Wisdom, in which she sings her song of love and warning. She tells of her role in Creation and in preserving creation. Christian theology has traditionally recognized the song of Wisdom as the song of Christ. This poignant poem speaks to the joy of God in creation.

> Ages ago I was set up,
>   at the first, before the
>   beginning of the earth.
> When there were no depths I
>   was brought forth,
>   when there were no springs
>   abounding with water.
> Before the mountains had been
>   shaped,
>   before the hills, I was brought
>   forth—
> when he had not yet made earth
>   and fields,
>   or the world's first bits of soil.
> When he established the
>   heavens, I was there,
>   when he drew a circle on the
>   face of the deep,

> when he made firm the skies
>> above,
> when he established the
>> fountains of the deep,
> when he assigned to the sea its
>> limit,
>> so that the waters might not
>> transgress his command,
> when he marked out the
>> foundations of the earth,
>> then I was beside him, like a
>> master worker;
> and I was daily his delight,
>> rejoicing before him always,
> rejoicing in his inhabited world
>> and delighting in the human race.

(Prov. 8:23–31)

If I cannot delight in the human race, I cannot be a pastor. If I do not have a sense of humor, I will be crippled in ministry. A pastor whose sense of delight and humor and joy has been taken away can never lead the people of God.

The issue of liking is the issue of leadership. Jesus' anointing became his friendship with sinners. He was Messiah in loving the unlovable; not just putting up with them but delighting in them; not for their sin but for God's image; for God's work of grace. If Jesus hadn't liked the people he served, he would have been a different god than the true God that saw all things good, that delighted in the human race in creation.

Not liking people is the personal guts of Gnosticism. Misanthropy is often a sign of its loathsome presence. Often, when a pastor begins to dislike the church, he or she will begin to spiritualize his or her call to that place. The more a pastor loathes the church and its people, the more he or she will retreat into spiritual isolation, away from the everyday concerns of parish life.

We may be able to theologize correctly about God's good will for a people we do not like, but we cannot lead real people toward God's good will unless we like them. They do not need to like us. That is the painful paradox of pastoral work.

Many times our people will not like us precisely in the area where we are doing our job correctly. But we must see and affirm the image of God in them; we must delight in what God delights in them; we must take pleasure in their presence.

People will follow us into God's good future if they see his love for them in our eyes.

The power of pastoral leadership is deliberately, stubbornly, and consistently liking people who do not necessarily like us. That means liking people who are not nice and who are not nice to us. Liking people who hate our guts is one of the great *agape* sacrifices of pastoral ministry. It is one of the hardest things any of us is called to do.

Liking the unlikables

The first step toward liking the people we serve is learning to like the church we serve. If we start by trying to like individuals, we get caught up in who we like more and who we like less, and that eventually turns into whose friendship we crave and whose we despise. It isn't hard to see where that could lead.

If we learn to like the church we serve, we can learn to like the people of the church for the sake of the church. Our personal friendships within the church must be kept in plumb with our friendship with the church. This keeps us working on the difficult relationships that we would not pursue except for the sake of the church. Focusing on the church *first* keeps our integrity intact in relationships with people we are tempted to like too much, particularly within the opposite sex.

But how do you to learn to like prickly, difficult churches?

I can only speak from experience. But I can positively say that I have learned to love, respect, and enjoy the small rural churches I have served (even the church that knew skunk were breeding under my office and didn't do anything about it) by seeking to understand the particular genius of each church. The four churches I have pastored have all been about 100 years old with dismal histories. Two of them remembered only one great pastor in their whole history. The others had no memory of a pastor whom they could say they loved and who stayed long enough to change much. The corporate self-image of each church mirrored fights and failures and timidity. They didn't know how to care for a pastor, and they weren't sure they wanted to know how. But the churches survived. They were the oldest private enterprises in each town by forty years; one of them may have been older than the local school.

Why did these churches survive? Setting aside for a moment the fact that one hundred years of struggle left the churches as cranky as Mr. Jones, how did they make it for as long as they did?

I became convinced that each of these churches possessed a particular genius, likened to the angels of the seven churches in the book of Revelation. I never called their genius the "church's angel." I understood theologically that God's Spirit preserved each church and that maybe angels were part of that. But I called it the church's "genius" because I wanted to know how God's providence worked its way through the corporate life of the people. I loved God for his work in preserving each church, but I wanted to know where God's preserving hand struck human gold.

It was a matter of finding the image of God in the church. Finding the image of God in Mr. Jones allowed us to love him, even to like him. Finding the image of God in the church allowed me to love my churches, and even like them, for what God had done through particular people with particular strengths.

This allowed me to affirm the strengths of each church, and it guided me in my pastoral leadership. The foolishness of attempting to pastor a church apart from its God-given genius should be obvious. Yet that is what many pastors, armed with briefcases filled with marked-up, underlined church-growth manuals, attempt to do to these little churches. Every old church is a book. It is an affront to the church and an embarrassment to the ministry when pastors read books *about* their church before they read the book that *is* their church. The problem is that when we read books about churches, we generally will compare that picture with the church we actually serve, and we will probably not like the church we serve. Obstacles to growth are all we will see.

The genius of a church is the secret to its growth. If you lead in the direction of the church's best self, the people will follow—most of the time. I must qualify this because a church's genius also contains its weaknesses and temptations.

Mr. Jones provides a perfect example of the genius of the church he attended. That church was the oldest private institution in the town. The town's bank probably took second place. It survived the Great Depression—one of the few that did in Montana. The reason was its tough, tight-fisted monetary policies that led to large cash reserves. The church had survived for 100 years because of kind, generous gospel policies, which led to large reserves of patience and understanding. The bank would have failed without its money policies. The times the church came closest to failing were the times it violated its gospel policies.

When the church loved Mr. Jones, it was doing what it did best. The ability to love that old coot was its genius. Its biggest battles took place when it violated what it did best. The church endured two bitter, church-splitting fights. One occurred in the late '70s when it refused to continue to allow the community senior citizens' lunch to use its fellowship hall and one in the early '90s when it refused to budge on the ball-cap issue. Besides the fact that there were legitimate sides to each issue, somehow, in each case, the church found a way to violate its own best self, and it paid a big price for doing so. That's why the fights were so huge. They were going contrary to what the church did so well. And, ironically, some of those who fought the hardest to remove the senior citizens' lunch from the church premises were the very ones who felt abandoned when the church would not accept boys in ball caps.

Churches rarely split over what they do poorly; they split over what they do well. Doctrine-oriented churches split over doctrine; fellowship-oriented churches split over fellowship; and mission-oriented churches split over mission. In its infancy, the fellowship-oriented, early church described in Acts 2 almost split over the distribution of food to Christian widows. Later it almost split over its Gentile mission in Antioch, and later, over doctrine.

When Mr. Jones's church was at its best, it was an accepting gospel lighthouse in the community. When it was at its worst, it fought over how to serve its own particular genius. How do you lead such a church? A pastor must know, understand, appreciate, and like its genius. If a pastor does not like the church, that pastor can forget leading it.

Do you voluntarily submit to someone who you know doesn't like you?

Pastors must discipline the church precisely on what it does best, not over the myriad things it does poorly and may never be able to accomplish. Unless, of course, he or she thinks that every church ought to be able to do everything well—and that invites the church to criticize the pastor's ministry for everything he or she does not do well—something we consider to be unfair and unkind.

The love of discipline

It may seem strange to discuss church discipline under the category of "liking the church." In ordinary life the people we like, our friends, are the people we find most difficult to rebuke. And yet, precisely with a friend, difficult advice goes deepest. The book of Proverbs talks about the invaluable function of our friends' disciplining us with correction:

- "Well meant are the wounds a friend inflicts, but profuse are the kisses of an enemy" (Prov. 27:6).
- "Perfume and incense bring joy to the heart, and the pleasantness of one's friend springs from his earnest counsel" (Prov. 27:9, NIV).
- "Iron sharpeneth iron; so a man sharpeneth the countenance of his friend" (Prov. 27:17, KJV).

Most of us don't pay much attention to the critique of people we know don't like us. However, we listen to our friends because we know they have our best interests in mind. But even deeper, we listen to our friends—even though doing so may hurt—because they know us at our best, they love us at our best, and they know when we are violating our own best self. No one but a friend knows when we are really hurting and when we need compassion, or when we are whining and need someone to kick us off the dead self-centeredness of self-pity.

Only a pastor who really likes a church can lead it in discipline. Only if we like a church are we able to see, appreciate, and affirm its strengths as well as truly understand its weaknesses.

This can be seen in the book of Revelation. Jesus tells the church in Laodicea, "I reprove and discipline those whom I love (*philo*). Be earnest, therefore, and repent" (Rev. 3:19).

Often the particular weaknesses of each of the churches in the seven letters to the seven churches in the book of Revelation are related to that church's strengths. To the church in Ephesus, John is told to write: "I also know that you are enduring patiently and bearing up for the sake of my name, and that you have not grown weary. But I have this against you, that you have abandoned the love you had at first" (Rev. 2:3–4).

But what about the prophetic role? Does a prophet need to like the people he or she prophesies to? Probably not. Jonah hated the Assyrians. But Jonah was not a pastor. Jeremiah cried buckets of tears over the objects of his bitter prophesies. He probably didn't like the Jews a whole lot. But again, Jeremiah was not a pastor. Isaiah, on the other hand, pastored and prophesied to kings. Still, "befriending and liking" Israel seems like an irrelevant category to apply to Isaiah. But there is a big difference between the word of prophetic judgment and the act of pastoral discipline. Jesus reserved the sharpest rebuke recorded in the Gospels for his dear friend Peter: "Get behind me, Satan!" (Mark 8:33). That was pastoral discipline. Jesus called the scribes and the Pharisees "broods of vipers and whitewashed tombs." That was prophetic judgment.

Pastoral discipline is more difficult to deliver than prophetic judgment. Pastoral discipline takes more guts, if only because it hurts so much more to be strung up by a friend than by an enemy. We can live without enemies. We cannot live without friends.

Most difficult of all is choosing to live in loyal bond with friends whom the Word, Spirit, and conscience force us to discipline. That is the sign of being a pastor. It doesn't feel nice. It requires the kind of pastoral love discussed in the next chapter: *agape*. The reader is forewarned: *agape* cannot be qualified by the word *nice*; *agape* is the least likable of all the pastoral loves. The model for *agape* is a prophet, Jeremiah's successor, the craziest man ever to wear the prophetic mantle: Ezekiel.

6

LOVE HURTS

THE NEW TESTAMENT LOVE-WORD *agape* has been so sanitized and compromised that we now have a word for love that we like. Of all the words for love studied so far, *agape* is the one word for love we shouldn't like. The other loves are different; we're supposed to like them.

The beautiful word *hesed* is the beautiful love: steadfast love. The gentle word *racham* is the gentle love: compassion. The delicious word *philos* has a great sandwich named after it: the philly cheese steak. These are all good loves. We can burn out showing all of them. But in their proper place and with the proper balance, these loves are supremely, satisfyingly human. They are also wonderfully divine.

But *agape* is a pain in the neck. *Agape* is brutal love.

Why else would the Greeks eschew this word? Was it because they knew what it really meant?

Yes, of course, because they knew that *agape* is the

99

love-word for absolute, unself-centered, brutal sacrifice. Its central meaning for the New Testament derives from Jesus' death on the cross: "For God so loved (*agapao*) the world that he gave his only Son, so that everyone who believes in him may not perish but may have eternal life" (John 3:16). This is about God sacrificing his Son. Steadfast love, compassion, and delight are all part of God's love for us, and they are all part of the sacrifice. But the sacrifice is *agape*. Jesus liked the sinners he spent time with; steadfast love was his only way of thinking; compassion for him was like breathing. But in his act of *agape*, his tone changed, and so did the tone of his disciples.

> Then he began to teach them that the Son of Man must undergo great suffering, and be rejected by the elders, the chief priests, and the scribes, and be killed, and after three days rise again. He said all this quite openly. And Peter took him aside and began to rebuke him. But turning and looking at his disciples, he rebuked Peter and said, "Get behind me, Satan! For you are setting your mind not on divine things but on human things." He called the crowd with his disciples and said to them, "If any want to become my followers, let them deny themselves and take up their cross and follow me. For those who want to save their life will lose it, and those who lose their life for my sake, and for the sake of the gospel, will save it. (Mark 8:31–35)

Peter, who adored Jesus' steadfast love and compassion, and who could never get over the fact that Jesus liked being with fishermen, tax collectors, and prostitutes, completely rejected Jesus' decision to act out *agape*. In his rejoinder to Peter's rebuke, Jesus called Peter "Satan." Jesus followed the admonishment with a lesson for all of us: "Deny yourselves, pick up your cross, and follow me." He never said we had to like it. He didn't like it when it became his turn to sacrifice. He partied with people he liked; he had compassion for people he healed; he promised never to leave or forsake his disciples. But when it came time for *agape*, he said: "Abba, Father, for you all things are possible; remove this cup from me; yet, not what I want, but what you want" (Mark 14:36). "At three o'clock Jesus cried out with a loud voice, 'Eloi, Eloi, lema sabachthani?' which means, 'My God, my God, why have you forsaken me?'" (Mark 15:34). That's the correct expression for living out *agape*: "My God, my God, why have you forsaken me?"

The apostle Paul's exhortation to *agape* is not a whole lot sweeter:

> If I give away all my possessions, and if I hand over my body so that I may boast, but do not have love, I gain nothing. Love is patient; love is kind; love is not envious or boastful or arrogant or rude. It does not insist on its own way; it is not irritable or resentful; it does not rejoice in wrongdoing, but rejoices in the truth. It bears all things, believes all things, hopes all things, endures all things. Love never ends. (1 Cor. 13:3–8)

Paul takes away our favorite sins—envy, boasting, arrogance, irritability, resentment. He requires us to make sacrifices for others but not for personal glory. He tells us that in this mess called "life," if our love is real, it "bears all things, believes all things, hopes all things, endures all things." I'm choking on the "alls." It gives an awful meaning to the phrase "love never ends" (or "never fails," as some versions render it). *Agape* hurts and exhausts.

The New Testament writers adopted *agape* as the standard word for love. We think this means that *agape* must also have some softer meanings besides "sacrifice," "death on a cross," "giving away our possessions and giving our body to be burned." But *agape* didn't make the Cross, the Cross made *agape*. The Cross isn't a subset of *agape, agape* is a subset of the Cross. The fact that the writers chose *agape* as the primary, defining word for love in the New Testament, and thus for life in the Christian community, shows how radically the New Testament redefines love from the perspective of the Cross. It also shows how radically the New Testament defines our concepts of friendship. For Jesus tells his disciples: "This is my commandment, that you love (*agape*) one another as I have loved you. No one has greater love than this, to lay down one's life for one's friends (*philos*)" (John 15:12–13).

Later, as his church foundered on the rocks of dissension, mistrust, and hatred, John told his flock: "In this is love, not that we loved God but that he loved us and sent his Son to be the atoning sacrifice for our sins. Beloved, since God loved us so much, we also ought to love one another" (1 John 4:10–11). And I have the audacity, before God and the whole universe, to ask, "I know I have to love (*agape*) my brother and sister in Christ, but do I have to like them?"

If we have *agape* for the people we serve, being loyal to them, having compassion for them, and liking them are a cinch. Jesus mustered the latter three loves without difficulty, but when faced with showing *agape*, he sweated blood.

As pastors we do not die on a cross for our people. The atoning sacrifice of Christ is complete. But there is a definite sense in which we follow in Christ's footsteps, as Paul did, who tells the Christians at Colossae that, "I am completing what is lacking in Christ's afflictions for the sake of his body, that is, the church" (Col. 1:24). Until Christ returns, we live out his *agape* sacrifice in the church, for the church, and for the lost world Christ came to save.

Redemption is complete, but a whole lot more love must still come to light. This love takes the Cross of Christ as its model, is an extension of it, and thereby brings Christ to the people to whom *agape* is revealed. For this reason Paul describes his life to the Christians in Corinth as "always carrying in the body the death of Jesus, so that the life of Jesus may also be made visible in our bodies. For while we live, we are always being given up to death for Jesus' sake, so that the life of Jesus may be made visible in our mortal flesh. So death is at work in us, but life in you" (2 Cor. 4:10–12).

Agape isn't so much its own kind of love as it is the other three loves rolled into one major sacrifice to accomplish the task of delivering God's love. Jesus' Cross is the ultimate expression of God's *hesed, racham,* and *philos,* but God's decision to send his Son to die and Jesus' decision to go the whole way with the sacrifice are *agape.*

Agape is decision love. *Agape* is the decision to make sacrifice. It is the decision to make deep personal sacrifice for the sake of the beloved. It is the decision to make sacrifice based on the realization that *hesed, racham,* and *philos* are not separate loves but unique facets of one love, the love of God who pours out his life for the world.

Tied down

Sacrificial love fleshes itself out in innumerable ways in pastoral work. But I am drawn to the sacrifice of Ezekiel for the people of Israel as a concrete definition of what it means for pastors to complete the sufferings of Jesus and thus bring him to people. The Lord told Ezekiel:

> And you, O mortal . . . lie on your left side, and place the punishment of the house of Israel upon it; you shall bear their punishment for the number of the days that you lie there. For I assign to you a number of days, three hundred ninety days, equal to the number of the years of their punishment; and so you shall bear the punishment of the house of Israel. When you have completed these, you shall lie down a second time, but on your right side, and bear the punishment of the house of Ju-

dah; forty days I assign you, one day for each year. You shall set your face toward the siege of Jerusalem, and with your arm bared you shall prophesy against it. See, I am putting cords on you so that you cannot turn from one side to the other until you have completed the days of your siege. (Ezek. 4:1–8)

God ordered Ezekiel to become a living parable of judgment. Pastors are living parables of love. But Ezekiel's prophetic tie-down was an act of *agape* as surely as was Jesus' and as surely as is ours. Beneath the judgment Ezekiel portrayed, his days roped to the ground were a type of Jesus' day nailed to the cross. Ezekiel's tie-down is a type of our years of commitment to the church we serve.

The fact is, many of us feel like Ezekiel. We feel tied by ropes to the church we love. We bond with it, but the bond feels broken; we have had compassion for it, but we feel burned out; we like it, but it has spurned our friendship so many times we strain to rejoice in it. If we choose to love in spite of the pain, that's *agape*.

For the pastor, the *agape* decision is the decision to stay put, to refuse to untie the ropes that tie us to the place God binds us, determined to show *hesed*, *racham*, and *philos* in a personal sacrifice far beyond the normal boundaries of these loves.

At this point, laypeople may cry foul:

- "We're stuck in our work too."
- "We're tied down to a job that hurts us."
- "That's just how it goes; tough it out."

- "Now you can relate to what we go through in the world."

Yes, but: Every other vocation works better with love, but does not strictly require it. Teachers, doctors, plumbers, politicians, and corporate types all do their jobs better if they love the people they work with, but they can do their job well enough without love because they are not paid to love people. In most jobs, integrity is defined by the ability to work for people we do not love. A surgeon who is acting professionally wouldn't flinch or slip stitching the guts of a person whose guts he or she hates. Any teacher can teach those he or she loves. The best teachers can teach people they thoroughly dislike. It's tough, but to be a professional demands learning to work with people you dislike.

Pastors cannot do pastoral work for people they hate or even dislike. Love is our life's work. We must love our church in order to do our job. The process of pastoral work for persons and churches we dislike or even hate is to learn to love those persons and churches.

"Impossible!" you say.

That's the point. That's why we must be tied down to the place we serve. And it is why staying tied down is our act of *agape. Agape*, like ministry itself, is radically free. We can choose to leave, and we can choose not to love. Often the two are the same decision.

The difference between *agape* and *hesed* is that *hesed* is covenant love and *agape* works above and beyond covenant obligation. What happens when the covenant is broken? The parties are set free. A pastor is free to leave a church that violates the pastoral contract, in letter or in spirit. *Agape* love is the pastor's decision to continue the bond beyond the ken of human bonding—when the covenant is broken and the parties are still bleeding. *Agape* is the decision to stay with the bond, continue living in *hesed*, long after the right to all *hesed* has been forfeited. This makes *agape* a radical form of freedom because it is always undeserved love. We say frequently and correctly that God did not need to send his Son to die for our sins. God sent his Son in freedom. It is likewise true that a pastor does not need to stay in a church and die for its foolishness. The pastor's choice is made in freedom. We can walk away and do well elsewhere. God will not curse our ministry if we do. But we can choose to stay. To choose to stay is *agape*.

Minority sacrifice

On the other hand, *agape* sets us free. Since the act of *agape* is the decision to make deep personal sacrifice, in that decision we absolutely transcend our circumstances—even as we are deciding to sink ourselves into our circumstances in a costly way. *Hesed, racham*, and *philos* are hard-wired into our human nature, and if our parents have raised us well, these loves are nurtured in us by a family and a culture that care about these loves. No individual, family, or culture can survive for long without loyalty, compassion, and friendship.

But *agape* is the decision to love to the point of giving our life away. *Agape* love transcends our human circumstances and instincts; it transcends our nature and our nurture. In this respect, to choose to make *agape* sacrifice is to make a decision utterly outside of human nature and nurture, and so it is utterly free.

A man who had just begun coming to church woke me from a deep sleep, after midnight, with a telephone call from a local truck stop.

"I'm really hurting," he said. "Can you come see me?"

"Can this wait for the morning?" It was the only rational sentence I could utter.

"No. It can't."

"Okay, I'll come down."

When I arrived and sat across from him in the booth, his first words were "You don't look like you want to be here." He spoke with obvious disappointment and a slight but definite edge of anger.

"I don't want to be here," I replied.

"Well, then, uh ... uh, why are you here?" he muttered. "What's the point—"

"Look—I'm here," I said. "Now what's on your mind?"

He was in great need, and the conversation was important. But I didn't need to feel compassion or friendship, and I certainly felt no steadfast love for him. I'd made the little but definite sacrifice to be there (at the time it seemed like a big deal). That's all that was required. I honestly felt then, and now, that I could have said no to the man and it would have been okay. I didn't feel a compulsion to go.

This is what the New Testament writers meant when they said that the community of Christ is a community of *agape*: We are to be a community in which we live and act in freedom—without fear. John tells us, "There is no fear in love, but perfect love casts out fear; for fear has to do with punishment, and whoever fears has not reached perfection in love" (1 John 4:18).

This is congruent with Paul's vision; we need no Law because where the Spirit of Christ rules, the reign of the Spirit is the kingdom of love: "Now the Lord is the Spirit, and where the Spirit of the Lord is, there is freedom" (2 Cor. 3:17). As we live in free sacrifice for one another, as we give our lives, we receive life back ten, twenty, and a hundredfold. *Agape* is our toughest choice in life, and it is also our best dream.

But, unfortunately, *agape* does not rule in the church. It did not in New Testament times (or Paul wouldn't have suffered as much at the hands of believers as he did at the hands of unbelievers). Though perhaps love has reigned for short periods in church history, no Christian community has come up with a way for Christians to live together in perfect love, and no one will until the Lord returns.

While it's okay to dream, in reality the church has always relied upon certain people to show *agape* even when the majority didn't. To be a pastor is to be one, among others, who chooses to make the sacrifice of love even when others won't. That means, in brutal terms, giving your life away to a community of people who, for the most part, are not going to give it back.

Agape is dangerous—to us and to those around

us. For one thing, our *agape* choices affect our families. Jesus guarded his decision to sacrifice, carefully choosing when and where to make his sacrifice. He did not readily give himself into the hands of humans.

Obedience-based sacrifice

How do we know when to choose *agape* in ministry?

Generalities are forbidden. We cannot trust our instincts. We can, for the most part, trust our instincts in *hesed, racham*, and *philos*; these we can understand because they are built into most of us and into our culture. But *agape* is "other" than us. It is a choice to be other than we are; that is, to violate our own nature for the transcendent freedom of the children of God.

As normal human beings who like life—the very thing the Scriptures expect of us—we cannot by nature be good at figuring out what our cross is and when we should pick it up.

We cannot use the concept of sacrifice as our criterion. That is, we cannot decide when and how to sacrifice simply because we perceive a sacrifice is there to be made. As 1 Corinthians notes, we can give all we have to the poor and deliver our bodies to be burned, but without *agape*, unless it is the right decision to sacrifice at the right time for the right reasons, the sacrifice is useless.

Martyr Jim Elliot could have sacrificed his resources to a soup kitchen on the way to South America and the Auca Indian tribe. Dorothy Day might have responded to a call to foreign missions, but then she never would have begun the Catholic Worker Movement with its gospel soup kitchens.

The criterion for the *agape* sacrifice is not the concept of sacrifice or even apparent human need. The criterion for *agape* is obedience to God. The Scripture says that to obey is better than sacrifice.

Since the coordinate of *agape* is obedience to God, *agape* frees the pastor from the church's social and psychological matrix, which can be so desperately stifling and, frankly, unnecessarily costly. *Agape* obedience may drive a pastor away from a costly, sacrificial ministry to a church that is a joy and a refreshment. For some pastors, this is the hardest sacrifice they can make.

How do we listen for God's will to sacrifice? We listen to it in freedom. We listen for his will knowing that we can walk away from the sacrifice and be happy serving him elsewhere. This means two things:

First, if we walk away from the sacrifice at a particular church and the future works out well for us, that doesn't mean that to have stayed at that church and made sacrifice was never really God's will for us. We can't have it both ways: if we want freedom, we need to accept responsibility for freedom. In other words, our lives may be happy doing something else, but our lives may not be as meaningful or as fulfilled as they might have been had we freely accepted the call to sacrifice.

Second, God gives us many opportunities to make the *agape* decision. Walking away once, twice, or even three times from churches that require the *agape* sacrifice does not preclude more spectacular opportunities to say yes to Christ's call to deny ourselves, pick up our cross, and follow him.

A word of caution: It is important to listen to God so that we do not waste our lives on sacrifices with no payoff for God (remember the parable of the talents?). Not every religious organization that uses the name "church" should have a pastor. Some (supposedly Christian) religious organizations house demons. They may confess good theology. They may be growing. The people may smile a lot. But they destroy pastors' lives.

Unfortunately you can't spot them easily; these organizations don't go by names like Belial Baptist, Conflagrational Congregational, or Profligate Episcopalian. The line between a church that needs a pastor and will support one—but needs lots of *agape* to survive—and a gang of thugs who can't abide pastoral care, kills pastors, and needs nothing but the dust from our feet, may be cracked and faded or virtually nonexistent. But Jesus orders us to walk away from pastor-killing churches. He's the *agape* man, but he also tells us: "Do not give what is holy to dogs; and do not throw your pearls before swine, or they will trample them under foot and turn and maul you" (Matt. 7:6).

Which brings us to the next chapter: the profile of a pastor-killing church.

7

"CHURCH" WITH NO LAMPSTAND

"SOME CHURCHES DON'T DESERVE A PASTOR," an old area minister told me. This fellow served our denomination in placement and conflict management, so he'd seen a lot. As a young pastor, I doubted him. I grew up in good churches.

Looking back, I can recognize there was conflict in the churches of my youth. But none of them split or, as far as I know, destroyed a pastor. During my college years, the pastors and churches in conflict that I observed conducted themselves appropriately—even in the midst of tension. God used the conflicts to advance the discipleship of these pastors and churches.

Following seminary, I worked as an associate pastor with a senior pastor who endured continuous conflict in a church that had a history of bad relationships with pastors. In his gutsy tenure of pure steadfast love, he outlasted many of the troublemakers and straightened many of those who had apathetically condoned the troublemakers over the years. The pastor who followed him has done well also.

So when I entered pastoral ministry, I believed, idealistically, that every religious organization that called itself a "church" and confessed a Christian theology truly was a church and deserved a pastor. I wasn't too receptive to my older friend's hard feelings about some of the "churches" he'd worked with.

But I remember, all too well, that when he talked to me about those "churches," his countenance transmogrified. His face reddened to scarlet. He winced. His pupils tightened. His gaze shifted from outward to inward, from the pleasant present to some vicious past. It reminded me of listening to veterans describe the horrors of combat.

He had the look of a soldier flashing back to a war crime: He saw a pastor's wife crying over her husband's mental breakdown. He saw a pastor perplexed by a church that cut his salary during a time of 12 percent inflation, while the local economy and the church parishioners thrived. He heard shouts and cries and curses at church meetings bubbling up as though from some deep level of hell. He remembered the cavalier tone of an elder as he recounted without emotion or shame how the last four pastors of that church had left the ministry.

I have never served such a "church," but I have talked with pastors who have, and now I am convinced that religious organizations do exist that merely *call* themselves "churches."

Hell's chaos

"Churches" such as these disembowel pastors. With words as sharp as knives, they slice open a pastor's soul until the *splaxna* gushes out. They rip open the pastor's *racham*. They take *philos* but they can not return it. They only know how to take. They are buckets without bottoms. No matter how much *hesed* you pour into them, it never hits bottom. They never fill up. They never overflow with love, mission, worship, or joy. *Agape* is wasted on them.

They come in all denominational flavors. They perjure themselves before the court of heaven when they confess their liberal, middle-of-the-road, or conservative theologies because they believe nothing. They hate God's anointed. They despise the lordship of Christ, and they despise his ambassadors. They are spiritual anarchists. They are "children of Belial," the Old Testament term for people of chaos.

The term *ben beliya'al* is a translator's nightmare. The King James translators chose the literal route by translating the Hebrew word *ben* as "son" or "children" but then transliterate the term *belial* to get "children of Belial." Modern translations replace the term completely with words from modern English. Generally, the *New International Version* translates the term as "troublemakers" and the *New Revised Standard Version* translates it as "scoundrels." Neither translation does justice, in my mind, to the characteristic of Belial as the power of chaos, anarchy, and death.

The following are some examples of what it means to be one of the children of Belial:

115

- "But some worthless fellows said [of Saul], 'How can this man save us?' They despised him and brought him no present" (1 Sam. 10:27).
- "Scoundrels from among you have gone out and led the inhabitants of the town astray, saying, 'Let us go and worship other gods,' whom you have not known" (Deut. 13:13).
- "Now the sons of Eli were scoundrels; they had no regard for the Lord" (1 Sam. 2:12).
- "Now a scoundrel named Sheba son of Bichri, a Benjaminite, happened to be there. He sounded the trumpet and cried out, 'We have no portion in David, no share in the son of Jesse! Everyone to your tents, O Israel!' " (2 Sam. 20:1).
- "The two scoundrels came in and sat opposite him; and the scoundrels brought a charge against Naboth, in the presence of the people, saying, 'Naboth cursed God and the king.' So they took him outside the city, and stoned him to death" (1 Kings 21:13).
- "And certain worthless scoundrels gathered around him and defied Rehoboam son of Solomon, when Rehoboam was young and irresolute and could not withstand them" (2 Chron. 13:7).
- "Do not be yoked together with unbelievers. For what do righteousness and wickedness have in common? Or what fellowship can light have with darkness? What harmony is there between Christ and Belial? What does a believer have in common with an unbeliever?" (2 Cor. 6:14–15, NIV).

In short, Belial is the power of death, destruction, and utter chaos working in the lives of people. Significantly, although the passage in 2 Corinthians speaks of unbelievers, in the context of the Old Testament, the children of Belial belong to the people of Israel. Virtually all of our churches have some children of Belial. Some persons are characterized by a bitterness that goes so deep that they are quite literally children of Belial. And to the extent that we have participated in party spirit and have sat in the seat of scoffers against other pastors (and which of us hasn't?), we too have imbibed of this demonic spirit.

Some religious organizations (which call themselves "churches") have drunk so deeply at the well of hatred that the entire "church" is controlled by this spirit of destruction. Whether these "churches" can be saved is up to the Lord. He may, in some circumstances, call a pastor to such a "church" with a special gift for delivering it from the legion that inhabits it. That is not my concern here. My point is that Jesus tells us that we must leave such religious organizations (which call themselves "churches").

Jesus wants us to sow the seed of the Word of God. And he teaches us that in our sowing, some of the seed will fall on the path, some will fall on rocky soil, some will fall into thorns, and some will fall into good soil. This is to be expected. This gospel parable is a source of encouragement. But Jesus does not want us to sow deliberately the seed of the Word into thorns. Some religious organizations (which call themselves "churches") are nothing but thorns.

Total abandonment

To pastors in these situations, Jesus says, as quoted in the previous chapter, "Do not give what is holy to dogs; and do not throw your pearls before swine, or they will trample them under foot and turn and maul you" (Matt. 7:6).

This familiar verse is not a law. It is a proverb. It is wisdom, but even more, it is permission. To pastors who insist on a course of self-destruction (giving their bodies to be burned but without love), it is a command. When Jesus sent out his disciples, he told them, "Whatever house you enter, stay there, and leave from there. Wherever they do not welcome you, as you are leaving that town shake the dust off your feet as a testimony against them" (Luke 9:4–5). In one region where the Pharisees attacked him vehemently, Jesus simply left: "The Pharisees came and began to argue with him, asking him for a sign from heaven, to test him. And he sighed deeply in his spirit and said, 'Why does this generation ask for a sign? Truly I tell you, no sign will be given to this generation.' And he left them, and getting into the boat again, he went across to the other side" (Mark 8:11–13).

So Jesus took his own advice.

Paul was forced to abandon religious organizations (which called themselves "synagogues"). Luke tells us:

> When Silas and Timothy arrived from Macedonia, Paul was occupied with proclaiming the word, testifying to the Jews that the Messiah was Jesus. When they opposed and re-

viled him, in protest he shook the dust from his clothes and said to them, "Your blood be on your own heads! I am innocent. From now on I will go to the Gentiles." Then he left the synagogue and went to the house of a man named Titius Justus, a worshiper of God; his house was next door to the synagogue. (Acts 18:5–7)

Later in Paul's ministry, some of his disciples and churches developed their own form of Christian children of Belial. Paul warns Timothy:

Alexander the coppersmith did me great harm; the Lord will pay him back for his deeds. You also must beware of him, for he strongly opposed our message. At my first defense no one came to my support, but all deserted me. May it not be counted against them! But the Lord stood by me and gave me strength, so that through me the message might be fully proclaimed and all the Gentiles might hear it. So I was rescued from the lion's mouth. The Lord will rescue me from every evil attack and save me for his heavenly kingdom. To him be the glory forever and ever. Amen. (2 Tim. 4: 14–18)

Sadly, "the lion's mouth" here is apparently "believers," persons who fully deserve the Old Testament title "children of Belial." Based on his experience with so-called Christians, Paul warns Titus, "After a first and second admonition, have nothing more to do with anyone who causes divisions, since you know that such a person is perverted and sinful, being self-condemned" (Titus 3:10–11). Paul is referring to church discipline. But when an entire church is filled with a spirit of divisiveness, the command applies to having nothing to do with such churches.

Finally, in the first of the seven letters to the seven churches, Jesus tells the church in Ephesus, "I have this against you, that you have abandoned the love (*agape*) you had at first" (Rev. 2:4). He admonishes them to regain their love at all costs because "I will come to you and remove your lampstand from its place, unless you repent" (Rev. 2:5).

Throughout this book, I have discussed the challenges I have faced in learning to love churches that offered little to commend themselves as objects of love except for this: at the heart of each was the Lampstand. Because of the presence of the Lampstand, all of these churches were genuine sources of light to their communities. However, in the case of the church in Ephesus, Jesus warns that it may lose the Lampstand.

Churches that lose the Lampstand become nothing more than a religious organization (which calls itself a "church"). Such groups do not deserve the love of a pastor. And they certainly do not deserve the chance to trample underfoot that which is holy or to maul God's pearls.

Many churches are simply difficult to pastor (and that I discuss in the next chapter). But the questions begging to be answered are:

- "How do you know the difference between a

'church' and a church?"
- "How do you know when you are throwing pearls before swine?"
- "How do you recognize a 'church' whose Lampstand has been removed?"

Lost Lampstand

Jesus tells Peter, "You are Peter, and on this rock I will build my church, and the gates of Hades will not prevail against it" (Matt. 16:18). Indeed, the gates of Hades will not prevail against the church in its gospel ministry until he returns. But the promise does not extend to every particular religious organization (that calls itself a "church"). Ephesus, an alive church, was in grave danger of losing its Lampstand, its share of the Rock upon which the church is built.

Each individual church must beware lest its gospel ambassadorship be taken away. Because if it is, the "church" will despise and destroy ambassadors of the gospel from that time forward. That is unless—by some miracle, which no pastor should take upon him- or herself to perform without specific direction from the Lord—that religious organization (which calls itself a "church") is restored to gospel ministry.

How can a pastor tell if a church has lost its Lampstand?

Three criteria come to mind. A "church" without the Lampstand:

- lacks the capacity to accept pastoral ministry that keeps the lamp burning;

- is indifferent to prayer;
- has a long history of raising its hand against God's anointed (and therefore can no longer bear the presence of the Spirit that anoints pastor and church for ministry).

Churches that lack the capacity to accept pastoral ministry are like sheep that refuse to be led to pasture; in the presence of food, they refuse to eat.

But when a pastor feeds his sheep with the Word of God, they shall not want. In loving leadership the pastor makes them lie down in green pastures and leads them beside still waters. In prayer and counsel the pastor restores their souls and leads them in right paths for Christ's sake. When the time comes for the sheep to walk through the darkest valley, the pastor is with them; the rod and staff of God comfort them. In obedience to the command of the Lord, the pastor administers the sacraments and prepares a table before them in the presence of their enemies; he or she anoints their heads with oil; their cup overflows. In giving them the love of God, goodness and mercy follow them all the days of their lives, and ultimately they will dwell in the house of the Lord forever.

This paraphrase of Psalm 23 is an idealized picture of pastoral ministry. But, keeping the parable of the sower in mind, the fact that not everyone experiences ministry in this way does not diminish the fact that some certainly do. We mess up plenty. We are often not faithful. But we strive to lead the flock to feed. Our ability to lead to feed is the measure of our ministry. A church is measured by its willingness to be led and fed. A church will receive the feeding of a pastor and will be nourished by it. A religious organization (which calls itself a "church") will not be led to food and will not eat.

A "church" indifferent to prayer is like a body indifferent to breathing; it is dead. We know from our battles with keeping personal devotions that prayer can become rote and lifeless, but we struggle back. When our spirit is weak in prayer, we gasp for Spirit-like lungs burning for oxygen after time under water. A religious organization (which calls itself a "church") feels no incongruity, no struggle, and no lung-burning as it proceeds with its pseudo-religious duties without prayer. It does not breathe, but it does not care. It is not alive. Its lamp does not burn.

"Churches" with long histories of lifting their hand against pastors cannot bear the presence of the Spirit that anoints for ministry. These churches defend their record of starving, boycotting, and firing pastors on the grounds that the pastors were all louts. Some of them were. But these churches forget that David refused to kill Saul in the cave. David did cut off a corner of Saul's robe, but even this made him feel guilty: "Afterward David was stricken to the heart because he had cut off a corner of Saul's cloak. He said to his men, 'The Lord forbid that I should do this thing to my lord, the Lord's anointed, to raise my hand against him; for he is the Lord's anointed'" (1 Sam. 24:5–6).

David had another chance to kill Saul, but he refused to allow Abishai to do so. He told Abishai, "Do not destroy him; for who can raise his hand against the Lord's anointed, and be guiltless?" (1 Sam. 26:9).

"Churches" are judged by God for the way they treat pastors like Saul, just as they are judged for the way they treat pastors like David. These "churches" apparently do not see that when they raise their hand against God's anointed—by cutting their salary or slicing away at their integrity with gossip—they are slashing at the very Spirit of God who has anointed the pastor. Eventually they will despise the Spirit of God, and as a result the lamp will go out.

It can be many years before a pastor or a denomination comes to the conclusion that a "church" will not take food and is indifferent to prayer. But the record of the destroyed lives of pastors is clear. It is a horrible thing to serve a "church" for several years, struggling for every gasp of air, only to have your face pushed again and again into putrid hogwash. If you dare to plunge your hand deeply enough in it, you will come up with crushed pearls and bone fragments of pastors who have been mauled.

When that happens, get out!

Denominations are beginning, finally, to keep track of "pastors" that sexually abuse parishioners. They offer them repentance and therapy or the door. If they don't, these religious functionaries (who call themselves "pastors") will continue to abuse parishioners in every parish they serve. When will denominations have the guts to do the same thing to pastor-abusing churches?

But the line between pastor-killing "churches" and churches that are difficult to pastor can be hard to discern. Such churches may have cut themselves off from pastors, they may have eaten from the Word sparingly, they may pray little, but there may still be hope. The Lamp flickers. Such churches, on the brink of death, still allows themselves to be prayed for. As long as a church allow this, it may be able to be pastored and loved. And through prayer it may be taught again to love the rich fare available to God's people.

8

RIDING THE BRAHMA BULL

ONE DAY WHILE JESUS, Peter, James, and John were on retreat on a mountain, the nine disciples left behind got into a hot fight with the scribes over ministry techniques. It seems the disciples botched an exorcism on a vicious, intractable demon that had possessed a boy for many years; the demon often cast the boy into fire and water.

The scribes observed the tragedy like a holiday and with perverse joy seized the opportunity to attack the disciples and, by inference, the entire mission of Jesus. The scribes questioned the integrity of the exorcisms the disciples claimed to perform up to that point. They splashed the Law—like acid—into the disciples' faces, citing Jesus' lax attitude toward the Law as the reason the devil withstood their ministry.

This forced the nine into a two-front war.

Outwardly the disciples defended their ministry while inwardly they questioned why their exorcism techniques failed. If they were at all like many pastors today, the disciples probably took a lot of the blame onto themselves—and secretly wondered if the scribes were right: maybe they needed to observe the Law better to get the ministry results they wanted. The demon controlled the argument by distracting the disputants away from the tortured boy and his exasperated father to generalities about the Law, demonology, and exorcism.

Meanwhile Jesus, Peter, James, and John had clambered up a mountain where Jesus was transfigured before them. He stood flanked by Elijah and Moses clothed in shimmering white raiment. The three great ones spoke amiably while the three disciples watched, confused and terrified. Thoroughly flummoxed, Peter felt a need to establish Transfiguration procedures. He suggested a building program as a way of preserving the experience. God interrupted Peter's misunderstanding by enveloping the mountain in a cloud. God spoke. It was like Sinai. But instead of receiving a new set of Ten, God told the disciples: "This is my Son, the Beloved; listen to him!" (Mark 9:7).

The event passed quickly. Walking down the mountain, Jesus told the three to keep quiet about what they'd seen, and he answered some questions. They asked him about scribal theology on the coming of Elijah, hoping he would tell them what he and Elijah talked about. They felt high at the sight of the three great figures, the light, the cloud, and the voice. It overwhelmed their minds. They felt prepared to change the world. But their glimpse of heaven did not change the fact that they were reentering a world of chaos and division.

They eventually came upon the nine disciples, the scribes, the crowd, and the argument. The crowd recognized Jesus as the solution to the roundabout, so they ran to him, leaving the scribes and the nine disciples without much of an audience.

Moses came down the mountain to debacles like this, Jesus must have thought to himself as he saw the crowd run toward him.

Peter, James, and John probably secretly relished the trouble the nine had gotten into: "Now it will be official. Jesus will install us as the top three disciples." Then they argued over which would rule the other two.

Of course Jesus did solve things—not with Law, but with faith and love. Jesus ignored what the devil found amusing—the religious fight—and went up to the boy's father. Jesus listened to the father, then he turned to the disciples and scribes and blasted them. It angered Jesus to see the boy ignored while the demon laughed. He exorcised the demon with force exceeding the power of the Transfiguration.

Later, the disciples asked Jesus why they couldn't drive that demon out. They'd succeeded in the recent past with some loose-knuckled demons, and this led them to believe they understood the ministry of exorcism. Thinking how happy they should be that they hadn't succeeded with that demon, since when it left the boy, it probably would have grabbed them by their necks and thrown them into a lake, Jesus calmly answered his disciples, "This kind can come out only through prayer" (Mark 9:29).

Thug or Brahma bull?

Some churches are possessed by spiritual dysfunctions as virulent as that demon. A religious organization (which calls itself a "church" but is really a gang of thugs) may be possessed by a demon or may be doing Satan's work so well that he leaves it to perverse paths of destruction. But a church possessed by a spiritual dysfunction doesn't have a real demon like a church of Belial may have; its spirit is the spiritual dysfunction of the gathered pain, anger, grudges, and fears of decades of gospel impotence and love failures. This spirit scatters pastors violently. This spirit makes the church leap, writhe, and spin, throwing pastors like an enraged bull pops cowboys into the air like tiddlywinks.

But these maladjusted centers for the worship of almighty God house angels. Their lampstand burns with a flame as stubborn against the night as any in Christendom. These churches brim with saints. Because individuals in these churches are so wonderful, ministry begins full of visions, dreams, and confidence. Our hopes may be backed up by some tangible gifts for ministry and a positive calling of the Holy Spirit. Bleary-eyed, we dismiss the fact—if we've even taken time to look at the church's past—that pastor after pastor has failed to make a dent in the church's circumstances.

Even if we know the church's past, we may feel

quite certain that we can succeed where no pastor has succeeded before. I know from personal experience that the devil loves this kind of pride because eventually it breaks our faith-grip on our call. The devil draws us into a two-front war: We can't fix the church, so conflict erupts in our ministry, just as it has in the ministry of almost every pastor for the previous sixty years. Outwardly we defend our ministry, inwardly we doubt it.

These inner conflicts weaken our sense of call to our church, and it weakens our sense of call to pastor *any* church, ever again. But if we hear Jesus tell us, "This kind can only be driven out by prayer," we may just ride the bull out. I once heard an old cowboy make a comment under his breath about a young man who'd just bragged he rode bulls in the rodeo: "A bull rider? That kid ain't no bull rider. His eyes ain't set close enough together to be a bull rider." I'll admit I've looked into the bathroom mirror the morning following a rough council meeting to see if my eyes were set close enough together to pastor the church. Sometimes a No. 2 pencil looks as thick as a rolling pin.

Then I get back on the bull and ride another day.

But this ain't no ride into a glorious sunset; this is a ride in an arena—the crowd, a cloud of witnesses and the church triumphant, is cheering, hoping this pastor has enough guts to ride the beast to the full count. Even the church cheers for us. The church wants us to win.

Here's the real difference between a church that's tough as a Brahma bull, but good deep down, and one that's a gang of thugs: The church that's tough, but good, will cheer for you and pray for you while you ride, hoping you'll succeed, while it's trying to throw you. The thug-church doodles with your mind for a time while it wires a bomb to your family car.

The difference is sort of like the difference between the demon-possessed boy and the scribes and Pharisees. Given the chance, the boy would have gone for the disciples' throats, hoping the whole time they could cure him. The scribes and the Pharisees on the other hand played games with Jesus and his disciples, waiting for the right moment to arm the bomb.

Prayer for howling spirits

How do you pastor a church that needs a pastor, deserves a pastor, desperately wants a pastor—a church in which most people hope you succeed but together can't help but try to destroy you? Do these churches need a pastor with well-honed administrative skills? With heat-seeking crisis management tools?

Not if the church is largely blue-collar—which is so often the case; these folks already despise the people in their workplace who get paid to manipulate them with strategies. And not if the church is largely middle-management, because middle-management folks already know all the strategies; they take pride in counter-managing to take the advantage. And not if the church is largely white-collar executives who resent sniveling bureaucrats trying to wangle promotions out of them. And if teachers and civil servants run the church, don't even think about trying to crisis-manage it.

Such churches usually operate inefficiently, and they appear to be poorly organized. But most church leaders run their businesses, offices, construction sites, classrooms, and homes quite competently. They can organize their home; why can't they organize their church?

Because in many instances, the leadership runs the church like the couple trying to push each other over the cliff of divorce runs their home—with an endless series of contradictory rules, boundaries, and agreements born of desperation and resentment. Common sense can't figure into it.

What they do not need is more rules.

They need less rules and more love. As they begin to love one another, the church begins to run better. To succeed in pastoral leadership in a tough church is to understand one simple principle of church organization and that principle's only vital but devilishly complicated corollary: Churches are not inherently complicated organizations.

Yes, churches do need good organization and competent administration, especially when a church grows or changes. But in reality, churches work best with simple leadership structures and simple programs. The spiritual dynamic in a church may be complex, yet the answer to this complexity is not more highly developed management but better prayer.

On the other hand, churches are bafflingly complex human-personal systems whose organization is complex in direct proportion to the historical dysfunction of the relationships in the church. The human-personal side of the church is highly complex. People are inherently complicated by the vagaries of human existence. When parishioners get locked into decades-long grudges, most of which are hidden beneath the surface of the church's everyday workings and often hidden to the wrestlers themselves, the church as a human system becomes virtually incomprehensible.

Still the answer is not more complicated church management. When the human-personal dynamic of a church is devastatingly complex, the church often attempts to hide the damage with increased administrative procedures. Simplifying the leadership and the program structures forces the people in the church to live their life together in love and in faith—that is to say, in prayer, listening to Jesus. This brings conflict to the surface where it can be dealt with. Another way to put it is that only prayer can cast out the howling spirits of dissension that snarl at every dream of succeeding in ministry.

Everything else needs to get done: preaching, calling, administration, sacraments, etc. But they cannot succeed unless prayer is the main tool of ministry. But here's the good thing: If you tell the church that you need to leave your office to go off and pray for them for an afternoon or a whole day, they are generally glad to let you do that. Why? Because they live in a bed in ICU, with nose tubes and heart monitors and catheterization. If you call on a church in the hospital, and you tell that church that they wouldn't be so sick if they just managed their church better (and you've got a great plan), they might just sock you in the mouth. If you tell that church that everything would be fine if all the members would just invite a friend to worship, the church will scream for the nurse to boot you out.

But if you gently ask the church if you can pray, it will be pleased as punch. That's because the church is sick, not bad. What kind of prayer helps? Only long, wrestling, agonistic love dialogues with God can cure this patient.

Long-wrestling prayer

It is far from simplistic to say that if a church is characterized by agony that her pastor's prayer life will be characterized by agony. Pastors who serve churches shot through with discord must pray through that discord and thus live through it. If it took a long time for the church to develop its deeply clever, covert misanthropy, it will take a long time for that distorted corporate psyche to be rectified by prayer. Such prayer can only be long, it can only be hard, and it can only be wandering; it requires a type of concentration bordering on free association. The couch may be a stream or a hay field or a mountain trail or the church sanctuary, but God listens quietly, making only slight comments along the way to micro-direct what often feels to the pastor like a meaning-less monologue.

The pastor who is bound in compassionate cov-enant with a church—which, in spite of so much, he or she delights to serve—will freely sacrifice countless hours to agonizing intercession with God and will be baptized into solidarity with the church, making *hesed* with it, suffering compassionately for it, grieving over its lost image of the body of Christ, and undergoing healing with the church, as a member of the church, in complicity with the church's sin. So this kind of prayer usually isn't pretty, but it is honest.

After all, the pastor is rarely an innocent by-stander in the church's escapades. Until in prayer we recognize our complicity in the human foolishness of our church, we can do no healing, no pastoring.

We come to the church as a hero. The church slices us and dices us. At that point we may leave, to wander the earth, to look for a church worthy of our heroism. Or we may join the church in her misery by recognizing our own. Sinful churches require sinful pastors saved by grace. Only pastors like this can understand churches like that.

What is our complicity with the church in its decades-long foolishness and failures?

Perhaps I should speak only for myself. My complicity in the crime comes at the beginning of the ministry, even before I accept the congregation's call. It comes as I willingly, gladly, joyously allow the congregation to seduce me into thinking that I am the pastor who can bring them new life. It's as if the church is saying, "Yes, I've had seven husbands, but I know that you are the one who has what it takes to make me happy."

And I believe the church. How is this possible?

Our whole system of pastoral training—from the

first affirmations of gifts for ministry to local church mentoring to academic theological education— stresses that with the right theology, the right skills, and enough charisma we can win over a church. I call it the Jim Morrison School for Pastoral Ministry— pastors are taught how to light the church's fire. Who doesn't want to be able to do that? Who will say no to a church that makes them believe they can do that?

What caused me to give up trying to fix the church by getting it enthused—and begin praying for it instead—was when I became acquainted with the pastors who had preceded me.

All were sharp, gifted, fine pastors. I was not more gifted than they were. I was not more committed than they were. I was not more spiritual than they were. And I was definitely not better with people than they were. Some of the parishioners preferred one or more of the previous pastors to me, and I could see why they did. When I saw how good the other pastors were, I said to myself, *I guess I'm number eight.*

I decided that all I could do for the church was pray. I decided to spend so much time praying that if the prayer was ineffective my ministry would fail. I still prepared rigorously for preaching, because the ministry of the Word needed to play a major role. And I still called on the sick and disabled people. But many things were simply left undone. I spent much of the time I would normally have spent trying to fix people, by praying for them. (Every time I went against that principle, the counseling failed.) I didn't spend much time *preparing* for council meetings; I spent time *praying* for council meetings. I didn't spend a lot of time showing laypeople how to do things in the church; I spent time praying that they could figure things out for themselves. This meant I had to let people fail (which some did), and then I had to take responsibility for the fact that they had not been trained properly to do their job.

If the prayer failed, the ministry failed. Then again, the way I figured it, if prayer doesn't work, what good is pastoral ministry anyway? If prayer doesn't work, then pastoral ministry is nothing but a chronically inflamed cultural appendix. So I stood to win either way. If long hours of praying worked, the ministry worked. If praying failed, that was fine too. I could quit pastoral work and join my former colleagues by getting a real job.

The prayer often felt so meaningless that I hoped that the project would fail. But the prayer worked. I found that I could not eject myself from the ministry by praying too much.

Long hours of prayer aren't easy. How do you pray all day? Prayer books seemed like they were written by super-intense, highly focused people who were a lot better Christians than I was. How could I do what they did? In school I was a goof-off. A daydreamer. A cutup. I have never successfully memorized a Bible verse intentionally in my life (I still need a Bible to quote Psalm 23 to parishioners).

How can something I'm so bad at be God's will for my ministry?

The number one misconception about long, hard prayer may come from our limited experience with it. We've tried it but feel like we fail so miserably at it.

But feeling miserably unsuccessful at long prayer is an essential part of the process. Probably no one is good at long, hard, wandering, wrestling prayer, just like no one is good at undergoing psychotherapy. Psychotherapy isn't any good until it makes us unbearably uncomfortable; as long as we are in control, we aren't being helped.

That's what this kind of prayer is like; if we're good at it, we aren't doing it. The whole point of long, hard, wandering prayer is to break down the pride that makes us just as enticed by the glory in fixing these churches as the nine disciples were by the glory they would have had if they'd been able to drive out the pernicious demon in front of the scribes and the crowd.

The only real intentionality in long prayer is to be there with God for the church.

Yes, I prayed for specific issues as they arose. But mostly I prayed for the whole church and for the church's pastor—one as guilty and as hurting as the church.

So a lot of this prayer is for mercy.

We ask for mercy only when we are desperate. With this kind of prayer, we begin by feeling desperate; that's why we go out to pray in the first place. But the prayer makes us feel only more desperate because when we try to pray all day and fail to maintain our concentration within the first five minutes, we lose confidence in our prayers—which is precisely what must happen. Only when we lose all confidence in our ability to pray do we really beg for mercy!

As long as we feel like we can pray we are still

playing the same old game.

The only way to pastor a church that has not been successfully pastored for twenty or even ninety years is to be the one who becomes absolutely positive that the church cannot be pastored except by prayer. Then ministry proceeds specifically on that basis. The minute I trust in my gifts—no matter how strong they are—I begin to die.

It's like being in a boat on a stormy lake and every gift we possess for rowing, anchoring, and balance mean nothing. All we can do is cry out, "Jesus, don't you care if we drown?"

He does care and he does calm the storm. Then he upbraids us for our lack of faith because the faith we had was a stupid mix of idealism, optimism, works-righteousness, and confidence in talent and hard work. Jesus tells us this in long prayer, and it humiliates us. And when we are humiliated, Jesus picks us up and gives us one more sermon, one more call, one more day to serve him. If we can string together enough one-day pastorates in a church, eventually we can look back and see them as a whole—in Christ. Looking back at eight years can seem like eight seconds.

Prayer for a tough little church

Deep in the heart of the ball-cap crisis (discussed in the first chapter), with only pain and no answers, I took a long walk in a suburban neighborhood of Spokane, Washington. My family and I were in town to visit my parents. The visit was almost over. After lunch we planned to get on Interstate 90 and head east for the four-hour drive home.

It was early Saturday morning, and some of the residents moved about their yards slowly, preparing for lawn rituals. This gave me some time in the cool air; I would not feel watched as I stubbed around the streets, talking to myself and to God. Rural people and urban people accept this activity as normal, but suburbanites seem to fear it; they band together to escape kooks. As I recall, I was barefoot.

Unable yet to see the deeper issues of the ball-cap situation, I was still mad at the church for rejecting a few good young men for wearing caps in worship. In the course of my wanderings through a newer section of the housing development, I came upon a nearly finished Mormon church. I broke the Tenth Commandment. In the context of thinking and praying about the trials of an old struggling church, I couldn't help but covet the new glass and the clean bricks and all the space! As I glared into the windows, I thought about the power of conformity in human systems. No one does sameness better than the Mormons.

Leering at a temple to homogeneity made me madder than ever at the situation in our church. *Are we going to be like them?* I wondered. *We can't.* At that moment, I did not ask myself about the price of diversity and whether there *ever* are boundaries. In the presence of that new Mormon church, I wanted something tidy.

So I walked and prayed and thought, chewing out the church as I masticated the issues. I defended the ball caps to the church in the theater of my mind—and, of course, my defense was brilliant (mental lawyering always is). I stopped to ask God if it was his will for me to blister the church the next morning from the pulpit. I had another sermon ready, of course; I served two rural churches at the time, so I needed a "regular" sermon for the other church anyway.

This long walk was one of those times when you really don't know what to do—when you ask God for direct guidance, hoping that the next thing that comes to mind will be the right thing, or that maybe one of the possibilities will carry special weight pointing to a solution.

The thought came strongly to me that I needed to put together another sermon that would level the church. However, another thought crossed my mind—quickly, like a hummingbird whirring over my head—*It won't do to preach the sermon with the boys and their families there. They would take it wrong.* But things had been so hot in church lately that the family had been gone camping most weekends—something they did every summer anyway. I was quite sure they'd be gone. But I did decide that if the boys were in church I would wait to preach the sermon.

So for the rest of my walk and for most of the drive home, I prepared a sermon as hot as an acetylene torch, praying the whole time.

On Sunday morning the "regular" sermon came off pretty well in the first church, especially considering that while I preached I rehearsed the "other" sermon in another part of my brain. I then drove to my other congregation, the one with the ball-cap crisis.

I remember walking up the wheelchair ramp at the church, desperately unsure of the next step but knowing that the future of the church might hang on the next few minutes. I opened the door, and who should greet me but the ball-cap boys. My face may have flushed red. I only remember looking down at the pages of my Bible and seeing two open spaces—one space contained the folded notes of the "regular" sermon and the other space contained the folded notes of the sermon inspired at the steps of the Mormon church building. I should have known all along which one I would end up preaching. That week the crisis began to turn in a different direction—I gained my first glimpse that the ball-cap dilemma was a control crisis and not a diversity crisis.

I can't tell you how glad I am that I did not preach that sermon—or how helpless I felt in the face of the fact that I nearly drove the church over a cliff—and that I was saved from doing it by circumstances completely beyond my control. So what good was the long prayer?

In the short run, the answer I "received" was dead wrong. I prayed and thought and schemed for about two hours, and the only fragment of truth that stuck in my mind was that I shouldn't preach the sermon if the family was there. But that was enough. In the process I worked through some pretty sore feelings, something I needed to do badly, and the Lord saved me from acting on them.

The real lesson was humility. I am little in control of my ministry if I am in such poor control of my own thoughts and feelings. I have to compensate in some way. Without a doubt the best venue for being an idiot is before the Lord; in some ways that is what long prayer is all about. Of course, the more crazy thoughts you have in your head, the longer you have to pray to sort them through.

Maybe those who pray shorter just have fewer brain cells devoted to foolishness (or maybe the lesson is to refrain from praying while coveting Mormon church buildings). But long prayer is the only way I know how to process the intricate crises that come from pastoring a tough little church whose pastor almost always thinks the wrong thing first ... second ... third....

And thus the need for long prayer.

9

PASTOR NARCISSUS

FLY-FISHING AND PASTORAL MINISTRY are like a Woody Allen movie: both are about sex and death, sex and death, sex and death.

Trout rise to eat the insects that ride the stream, suspended on the surface tension of the water. The insects are on their way to mating, fertilization, and then death. The fly-fisher floats a fur-and-feather imitation of the insects on the surface of the water, hoping to trick the trout into a strike. The trout must eat the bug to live. The bug must reproduce to prolong the existence of the species. The fisher interrupts the fish's feeding cycle by catching it. The fateful meeting of the fisher and the trout are keyed to the reproduction-and-death cycle of the insect.

Pastoral ministry is, likewise, to a large degree keyed to the reproduction and the death cycles of humans. This is the natural relation of the cycle of *eros* and *thanatos*, the Greek words for sexual love and death. We conduct ceremonies for the purpose of solemnizing and blessing the birth of humans, the onset of puberty in humans, the mating rituals of humans, and the death of humans. Much of the church's ministry is organized around the orderly and successful progress of reproduction cycles. We initiate programs to support and enhance courtship, marriage, and child raising. We devise youth groups, one major purpose of which is to keep humans from mating too soon. The modern church attempts to provide program niches for persons not directly involved in the reproduction cycle—singles and seniors—but the church is never as good at that as it is at providing program support for those intimately involved in human reproduction.

Why?

One reason may be that the church and its rituals evolved over a couple thousand years during which successful reproduction was continually threatened by high infant mortality rates and short life expectancy. For instance, the purpose of the genealogies in the Bible is, at the very least, to demonstrate God's providential care of humanity. God provides for the preservation of humanity generation after generation. In its reproduction rituals, the church affirms and blesses what the genealogies demonstrate.

The church's involvement in confessing and providing God's blessing on reproduction goes back thousands of years. It is not less important today. People care only a bit less today about obtaining divine blessing upon marriage and reproduction than they did before. Case in point: modern Europe. Virtually the entire native, Caucasian, atheist/agnostic population is baptized. As a pastor I can say without the slightest hesitation that nonbelievers are often more insistent on the importance of religious ceremonies to begin marriage and to usher in infancy than are believers.

So the church and its rituals are shot through with *eros*. Many of the church's oldest rituals solemnize *eros*, regulate it, even glorify it. Pastors hope that there's plenty of *eros* in the marriages in the church. Parish life goes better when marriages are healthy. (The marriage-seminar industry may not, since when marriage is hot their business is not.)

The church is also shot through with *thanatos*. We deal constantly with death issues and particularly with helping people not to fear death. Again, many of the church's oldest and most venerable rituals solemnize *thanatos*, regulate it, and glorify its defeat.

Fatal attraction

The church acknowledges the proper place of *eros* in life and it regulates it. But we state unequivocally that *eros* has absolutely no proper role in the relationship between pastor and parishioner, and it has no proper place in the relationship between the pastor and the corporate body of the church. The result of erotic involvement is always some form of *thanatos*, for the parishioner and his or her family, for the pastor and his or her family, and for the whole church.

At least part of the problem is, however, that *eros* thrives in the environment of the true pastoral loves:

hesed (loyalty, bonding), *racham* (compassion), *philos* (delight and friendship), and *agape* (sacrificial love). Frankly, bonding to a person of the opposite sex with compassion, delight, and sacrifice is for most humans an aphrodisiac. Pastors who show real pastoral love can, without great care, become ecclesiastically aroused. Believe it or not, pastors can love the whole church erotically.

When pastors build the church on the basis of erotic love for the organization, the next (perversely logical) step is for the pastor to love a parishioner erotically. Often pastors who do this don't see anything wrong with it until they are confronted. The reason that loving parishioners erotically doesn't seem wrong to some pastors is because they have spent so many years loving the *church* erotically that loving a parishioner erotically is a perversely logical form of discipleship. It is shocking how many pastoral sexual affairs start out as pseudo-discipleship, and continue on that basis:

> They acted shamefully, they committed abomination; yet they were not at all ashamed, they did not know how to blush. Therefore they shall fall among those who fall; at the time when I punish them, they shall be overthrown, says the Lord. (Jer. 8:12)

What does it mean to love a church erotically?

First, the argument of this book is that the pastor can love and must love the whole church, not just the individual parishioners. Now if a pastor can love a church with *hesed, racham, philos,* and *agape*, it may well be possible, even if it is wrong, for a pastor to love the whole church with a kind of *eros*.

Second, the church is by its nature an erotically charged environment—it affirms, regulates, and blesses *eros* in its proper place—which makes the possibility that the pastor could love the church with *eros* quite conceivable.

Third, the obvious truth that the four great loves of pastoral ministry are also the four great loves of marriage—and that the exercise of these loves makes the pastor a possible object of erotic attraction for parishioners—increases the possibility that the pastor may covertly substitute *eros* in pastoral work.

Still, the idea that we can have an erotic attachment to a church may seem far-fetched. But consider this: Pastors commonly use erotic terminology to describe the effect of their ministry. Pastors say they want to excite the church, or turn the church on, or even light the church's fire (The Jim Morrison School of Ministry).

Most of us want to lead exciting worship and preach on-fire sermons. Many parishioners want us to. When pastors deliberately set out to excite their congregation in worship and preaching, what is getting excited? Are we only exciting parishioners spiritually?

But what are we really talking about?

Nothing more than good, old, all-American narcissism, a bastard love that has no place in pastoral work.

Pastor Narcissus

The story is told that Narcissus, a son of a nymph, flirted injuriously with the affections of the nymph Echo. Echo eventually pined away to become nothing more than a disembodied voice. Narcissus, bent on further pseudo-conquest, messed with the mind of another nymph, who tattled on him to a powerful god named Nemesis. Narcissus' nemesis became his love for his own image. One day, wandering in the forest, he came upon a pool of water into which he glanced. Narcissus saw his own image, became fixed to it, and could not break away. He died beside that pool—in love with himself.

This story is told over and over in pastoral ministry: Pastor Narcissus is in love with himself; that is, he is erotically in love with his church, which he sees as an extension of himself. This is seen in two ways:

First, Pastor Narcissus is attached to his image in the pool of the church. Pastor Narcissus is attracted to the visage of the whole church as it is being built under his leadership. What great things he has done! These things reflect well on him. There is much yet to be done, but he is determined to continue to build the church according to his vision. Anyone who stands in the way is dispensable on account of a greater good, which is the enlargement of the pastor's image.

Eros may seem a strong or odd term to apply to a pastor's love for what he sees of himself in the church. But none of the other loves fits. *Philos* comes close, but *philos* for a church is love for what God has made the church to be; it delights in God's goodness for the sake of the church, not for possession, self-aggrandizement, or personal enjoyment.

Erotic love for a church, on the other hand, is a form of possession of the church. It is love for the aggrandizement of self in ministry and for the pastor's image, which he has foisted upon the church. It is to be tempted by possession, self-aggrandizement, and personal enjoyment to dearly hope our church will "make us proud."

Second, Pastor Narcissus lacks boundaries. He doesn't know where he ends and the church begins. By fixing his gaze upon the church as an image of himself, Pastor Narcissus sees the church as, at the very least, an extension of himself. He sees the church and its individual parishioners as something he wants and as something he cannot live without. He is attached to it and to them as if by an umbilical cord. The line between what Pastor Narcissus *makes* and what nourishes him simply disappears. If Pastor Narcissus takes the credit for making the church, then most surely he takes credit for the fact that the church provides for him. Eventually he cannot imagine life apart from the church he has made and its nourishment.

If Pastor Narcissus thinks he needs or wants sexual attention, he simply takes it. He takes it from himself for himself. After all he built it—it is his, he needs it, he deserves it. This is bogus-*eros* and has nothing to do with adult sexual love. Pastor Narcissus is not looking for love or adrenaline; he seeks death. Sex with a parishioner is an escape into certain death.

We must never believe a pastor or a parishioner who has been involved sexually when he or she says: "We didn't mean to hurt anyone." In Proverbs, wisdom tells us, "Those who miss me injure themselves; all who hate me love death" (Prov. 8:36).

Narcissistic attachments are deep and primitive, and probably all of us who pastor struggle with them on some level. The question is how this crazy stuff gets out of control.

The answer, I believe, is ambivalence.

I discussed ambivalence earlier in this book as the numb state of existence pastors fall into when, through the pounding they receive in ministry, they don't feel they can risk love again. Love is dangerous.

But ministry can't be done without some kind of love. So ambivalence retreats into self-love and self-protection. To put it in psychological terms, when ambivalence takes over a ministry, the pastor's inner child becomes the pastor of the church. Obviously this happens a lot. Laypeople can attest to how intractably childish some pastors can behave. Of course, these same laypeople don't recognize that the blows they deliver on a regular basis force the pastor into primal retreat.

Whereas bitterness causes pastors to put up barbed-wire fences, ambivalence can break down a pastor's sense of personal boundaries. The blows come from every side, and eventually the pastor simply lays down the fists and gives in to the attack. Sadly, ambivalence sees death as a reasonable solution. As the defenses go down and the will to live lessens, merging into some kind of peaceful place without pain can sound good. So can getting forced out of the ministry through having an affair—a form of death.

The sorry, wimpy state of the ambivalent pastor hardly seems to fit the picture of the lusty, selfish, church-building, parishioner-abusing Pastor Narcissus. But they are definitely the same person. That abused children can become weak adults who abuse children is quite suggestive to this discussion. That powerless, ambivalent adults are frequently violent suggests the same. So does the sad truth that when we are weakened by life's beatings, we often find it difficult to live by our most dearly held values. This is a good enough reason to leave a pastor-killing church or any church that pummels its pastor to the point of childish, moral weakness.

Whether outwardly successful in ministry or not, often Pastor Narcissus is a pastor who has been beaten up many times in life and in ministry. It is sad, but it is no excuse. Pastors can choose not to become ambivalent in ministry by, among other things, choosing to love the church properly as an adult or by leaving the church.

And though the pastor cannot help but administer the ceremonies of the sex-and-death drama of the church, the pastor can and must transcend that drama or perish in it. The pastor cannot escape involvement in the sex-and-death drama in the church but can transcend the drama professionally—clerically—in a manner similar to the way a fly-fisher is involved in but still transcends the sex-and-death drama of the trout stream.

The fly-fisher's involvement is from the outside. The fly-fisher uses the tools of fly-fishing—the fly rod, the line, the reel, the artificial fly—to involve himself or herself in the sex-and-death drama of the trout stream. The tools of fly-fishing are the logical but objective extensions of the fly-fisher to catch the trout. The fly-fisher does not jump into the water and grab the fish by the gills.

The pastor uses the tools of ministry to affirm, regulate, and bless the sex-and-death drama of parish life: the Word and the sacrament. To the extent the pastor's exercise of these tools represents genuine pastoral love and the desire to bring men and women to obedience to Christ, they are the logical but objective extension of the pastor into the sex-and-death drama of the parish.

But there is a line pastors cross, where they stop exercising the ordinances modestly. They get cute, original, and personal with the biblically ordained tools of ministry. They inject themselves into the ceremonies they perform, the sermons they preach, and their calling. This is a crossing of personal boundaries into the sacred arena. Whenever a pastor performs ministry in a way that makes it seem like his personal involvement is more important than the ceremony itself—as if without his vital, personal input this sacrament is flat and ineffective—I wonder if Pastor Narcissus isn't at work.

When the pastor stops ministering Christ and the love of Christ and ministers himself and his own love, the pastor's life is no longer the parable of Christ; the pastor's life is the "thing" itself. When the pastor/parishioner relationship becomes the parish cult, Narcissus' invasion of the parish is complete; all that remains is for Pastor Narcissus to dive into the bottomless pool and die.

As vital as they are to pastoral ministry, personal relationships between pastor and parishioner are not actually the pastoral ministry. The pastoral ministry is the communication and administration of Christ in Word, sacrament, and in the pastoral relationship, which is indeed personal but is much more and much different than merely a personal relationship. The pastoral relationship is a specific kind of personal relationship that exists within the community of the church, is governed by its order, and, by various ordained means, communicates the transforming love of Christ.

This brings me back to the importance of *agape* to ministry. Pastoral relationships that are not governed by the *agape* love of Christ for the parishioner and the *agape* love of the pastor for Christ will always degenerate into a destructive form of personal love, which is not pastoral love. The pastor's *agape* love for God is the free, transcendent decision of the pastor to love the church sacrificially for the sake of Christ and not for the pastor's own glory.

The pastor's *agape* love is first and foremost love for God. We must love God first, and then our church and our parishioners for the sake of our love for Christ. Only in this way can Christ stay at the center of the church, instead of the pastor moving to the center of the church. The church must be the body of Christ. It must reflect his love, project his image, and be his witness to the world. The pastor is the servant of this love, this image, this witness.

10

WHAT'S A PASTOR FOR?

I KNEW SHE CHOPPED her own wood, but I'd never seen a ninety-pound, ninety-four-year-old blind woman swing an axe before.

Driving up unnoticed, I stopped to watch. Like a praying mantis covered in draping rags, Kathryn stooped over her chopping block. Sure-handed, she sliced kindling from a round of dry lodgepole pine with her axe. Transfixed, I sat motionless. I was no longer conscious of time; I could have been anywhere at any time in history. This was life hanging on in the most basic sense.

Kathryn burned the wood in her kitchen stove. She boiled water fetched from the ditch beside her house. She was fiercely independent. It took three years of visiting before she'd let me chop and stack wood for her.

Once a month I bring the Lord's Supper to a few shut-ins. Willa, a retired woman from the congregation, is my intrepid companion and goad. She reminds me when it's time to go out and serve our shut-ins again. She lovingly prepares the Communion kit.

Kathryn is one of our stops. Poised erect on the edge of her chair, wearing a straw cowboy hat discarded by a child, and staring forward, Kathryn talks. Like the lawyer she might have been in another era, she gives us practiced diatribes. For years she has lived alone. For countless hours she has murmured to herself the great truths of her life. She knows that Christians, especially pastors, are a long-suffering audience. Her head is thoroughly packed with opinions. She has no room for anyone else's.

"The problem with people today," begins Kathryn, "is that people do not wear enough natural fibers. Cotton and wool—that's all I ever wear. Nylon is bad for the heart and causes arthritis. People should stop wearing these new fabrics and wear cotton and wool. I daresay there'd be no need for doctors if everyone wore wool."

Not missing a beat, she continues, "I've never been to the doctor in my life, and I never intend to go to one. No, if people would just use common sense there'd be no need for doctors. We all just need to wear wool." Since she enjoys near-perfect health, it's hard to argue with her.

When I can bear it no longer, I usually interrupt, "Kathryn, now I am going to read the Bible, and we will have the Lord's Supper."

"Okay," she says. She stops talking and waits silently, obediently, unguardedly. As usual, Kathryn appears to merely tolerate our agenda. In this context, that's a compliment. If our presence displeased her, she'd let us know. Once I made the mistake of trying to put my arm around her.

"I don't believe in love!" she retorted, squirreling away from me.

But then, on another occasion, I read Psalm 23: "The Lord is my shepherd, I shall not want. . . ." Looking up after the reading, I saw a sight rarer than a ninety-four-year-old blind woman chopping wood. Kathryn, the highly self-controlled survivor, was weeping and tender; she had been touched directly by God.

I think she was touched by God every time we came. I think the tears were a fissure opened up to show us what was happening inside.

This is pastoral ministry in the most basic sense—friendship, the Word, prayer, and the sacrament come together to deliver to her the presence of God.

Axe to the core

I'm good with an axe. I can dispatch the lever edge of a ten-pound splitting maul to the heart of a round of wood with power and accuracy. It takes confidence and skill to swing an axe with all your might. If you miss the core, you risk glancing the axe off the log; it's easy to bloody your shin.

Sometimes, when I'm pastoring with all my might, I feel as if I'm glancing off the side of the task instead of hitting the center. I feel blood on the inside of my pant leg. I know then I need to correct my aim. I need better vision. True pastoral ministry isn't always easy to line up and strike with precision. It takes practice and experience.

Kathryn can swing an axe blind because she chopped wood for eighty years with sight. I'm starting out swinging blind. Furthermore, Kathryn's round of lodgepole pine sits still on her chopping block. My tasks spin in my head like Dorothy's farm caught in the vortex of a Kansas twister. I can see them but I can't touch them. I feel no direction.

In my more lucid moments, I see the tasks of my calling like pictures on a wall. They're all lined up waiting. To choose one I just step into it. For sermon preparation, I see a stack of books with paper and pencil. For calling I see a closed door that I'm supposed to knock on. For administrative work I see a desk cluttered with rough-torn opened envelopes. For praying I see a worn, bare, dirt trail winding through wild grasses, woods, and rivers that I can meander through.

When I step into a task, I see a list. The list is a technological description of the proper way to complete the task. For sermon preparation, the first instruction I see tells me to do textual criticism on the Masoretic text of my sermon passage, comparing it with its Septuagintal counterpart. I'm not bad with Hebrew and Greek, but textual criticism is part of another life a long time ago in seminary. I can't seem to shake demands.

Each list has gaps. I've learned a lot from veteran pastors, personal experience, and reading, but when I'm honest with myself I don't feel very smart about any of these tasks.

When I step into the calling task, I see great ideas that worked once and failed every time thereafter. I don't feel secure in my pastoral-calling technology. I've called on plenty of people, and they never came to church again. But I also remember that I have visited some people and God has been there. And who's to say that God hasn't been present in the visits when people never came back?

I know this: Bible reading is a powerful force in calling. When I read the Bible, God comes. When I read the Bible during a pastoral call, God enters the room. Sometimes we all are shaken up.

A pastor must be someone who goes around and reads the Bible to people.

"I'm afraid to die," Kathryn says. This is one of Kathryn's nagging fears.

"I can't imagine what God will do with a skunk like me," she goes on. I lower my tenor voice to a pastoral timbre and give her a lecture on Reformed theology—salvation by grace through faith, the death of Jesus, the forgiveness of sins, the resurrection of the dead.

"I'm not afraid of Jesus," she says. "It's God I'm not sure of. Jesus is one thing, God is another. I don't know what God will be like when I meet him."

Not certain what to say, I change the subject.

"Where did you live as a child?" I ask her.

"We lived on a farm in Alberta, Canada," she says. "We raised all kinds of animals and grains. Father was a wonderful, hardworking man."

"Do you have any strong memories of those days?"

"Oh yes," she says and pauses. "I remember once when I was seven years old my father was driving a large mule-drawn wagon by the house. My little sissy Bess was only about two. Somehow or other she waddled out, and without my father seeing her she got herself under the wheels of the wagon. My father drove right over her."

I gasp.

"The wagon wheels rolled right over the diapers, and she wasn't hurt at all. Those diapers saved her life. I never saw the likes of it. I remember it now just like it happened yesterday."

I read the Scriptures and pray while Willa prepares the Lord's Supper and serves it around. Before the words of institution, I say, "Kathryn, Jesus is like Bessie's baby diapers. These elements, the broken body of Jesus and the shed blood of Jesus are Bessie's diapers . . . they wrap us up in the love of Jesus and they save us."

Kathryn cocks her head slightly downward and gives a quick inward laugh. She is peering within. Something is happening. The Holy Spirit is administering the death and resurrection of Jesus to her; she experiences firsthand the steadfast love of the Father. Her joy bubbles outward. She smiles as she takes the elements. They are a sign of an inward grace.

She rarely comments on being afraid to die after that.

Wood-splitting sacrament

What is a pastor?

One part of my pastoral life can't be right: this

nagging sense that my ministry is constantly on the brink of total collapse. It's irrational. I'm liked and respected. I have a theology of God's love, Christ's acceptance, and the Holy Spirit's guidance in my life. I need a good dose of my own theology, but it stays stuck in my head where it isn't doing me much good.

I'm still a child. I need simple pictures of God's love. I need transparent parables, symbols that are obvious. When I receive the Lord's Supper, I see Jesus with my eyes as the elements are passed to me. I reach out to hold them. I feel Jesus with my fingers as I tenderly grasp the bread and cup and raise them to my lips. I smell Jesus with my nose as molecules spin off the bread and the juice into my nostrils. I taste Jesus with my tongue and even hear Jesus as my jaws creak into action, and my teeth masticate the elements. When the story of the Atonement comes to me in the symbols of the Lord's Supper, God enters and changes my thinking.

Slowly it sinks in, but only through the simplest symbols of God's love. That's how my theology gets inside me.

Kathryn and I are in the same boat. We have the same Savior mediated to us in the same way.

I administer the simple symbols and parables that bring Jesus to people and make them unafraid of God. A pastor is someone who brings the Lord to people through administering the Lord's Supper.

Entering Kathryn's house, Willa and I are assaulted by her tiny one-eyed dog and the smell of its feces. Dirty dishes are everywhere. Envelopes opened and unopened, bills paid and unpaid, discarded eyeglasses, squished tubes of salve, and a broken television litter her table in the middle of her front room.

People from town come by and try to help, but the work is slow, and Kathryn accepts little or no help. A few people she selects bring her water in plastic jugs in the winter when the ditch is frozen. If she's in a good mood, she'll accept a box of food from the church.

One day I tentatively approached her with a suggestion: "Kathryn, have you ever considered receiving Meals on Wheels? It's good, hot food, and the people will deliver it right to your door."

Her face wizened as she gathered her wits. "That's one step away from the garbage can!" she declared. (I am about one inch from being ordered out of her house.)

Retreating just a little, I asked, "What's the garbage can?"

"The rest home," she said. "And you see, once you start taking help, then they have you. It's always your own people, your own family that will do you in. They'll turn their back on you and get rid of you. I've seen it many, many times. Don't think for a minute that I don't know what they'd like to do with me."

"But Kathryn, don't you know that there are a lot of people who love you?"

"I don't believe in love," she snapped. "The word *love* isn't in the Bible. The Bible calls it 'charity.' That's what I believe in, charity. Anyway, your own folks don't have charity for old people anymore. They want us in the garbage can to be rid of us. It's just that simple."

The conversation ends. Again, there's not too much to argue with.

Kathryn has no immediate family. She was married once, no children: "Harry and I went our own way a long time ago. We never divorced; I don't believe in it." Her only relatives lived in Alberta, Canada: a sister and her sister's daughter. Her niece came down and tried to help, but rarely got further than we did. No one could consistently help Kathryn with anything.

It was getting cold and icy outside. Inside, Willa and I saw that Kathryn was out of wood. She was agitated. Less stable on her feet, she wasn't able to get wood like she used to. She mentioned taking some falls in her house. I broached forbidden territory.

"Kathryn, could I get you some wood?"

"Don't bother yourself with it," she returned.

As stubborn as she was, I kept pestering her, "I'd really like to get you some, if I could."

"Suit yourself," she said.

Feeling as if I'd been granted entrance to the royal court, I skipped outside. For the next several hours, I chopped and hauled and chopped and hauled.

"How does this look, Kathryn?"

I held out an armload of fresh-split lodgepole. She fingered the wood and laughed derisively. "Those are saw-logs to me. I need it split much finer than that!"

I re-split it. Forty-five minutes later there was as much wood stacked in her front room as she would allow.

Kathryn began to thaw a little. She accepted hot

meals from people in the church and even accepted
Meals on Wheels. People began to help her with her
bills. Her niece and some others cleaned her place up.

It was the warmest winter on record, and a storm
was coming in. By 4:30 P.M., the temperature was
dropping by the minute, the wind screaming. The
chill factor was about 20° below zero. We were headed
for a week of sub-zero temperatures. On my way
home from the office, I stopped by Kathryn's. Once
again she was out of wood. Chop and haul, chop and
haul. Standing in her doorway, she stared in my general direction as I returned to my truck. Somehow
through wood-splitting, God came to Kathryn.

Ambition abolitionist

I call what I do "friendship." I have a toolbox. If
any of my friends need help, I pull out any tool I have
and try to use it to help my friends. I don't think pastors are meant to be psychologists, but I know a little
about psychology and I'll use it. I know a little about
life in the Spirit—that's a tool too; I try to help people
learn how to pray. I know a little about Christian morality, and I'm not afraid to confront a friend with the
truth. I can listen to a person in distress. I can visit
someone in a hospital and hold her hand while she
endures a seizure. I can play a little basketball with
some friends or go fishing with a buddy. I can swing
an axe.

Jesus was accused of being a friend to sinners,
and rightly so. To his opponents, his friendship with
outcasts was his blasphemy; to Jesus, it was his call-

ing. Those he chose as friends, he listened to, answered, loved, helped, healed, challenged, and spent time with. For Jesus, this accomplished something like what psychologists attempt to do: He helped people find wholeness.

Friendship is not a profession. It isn't even necessary for everyone. We say, sentimentally, that people need friends. But Kathryn, for close to ninety years, proved she really didn't need friends. Kierkegaard said, "A friend is not what we philosophers call the necessary other, but the superfluous other."

Psychologists are necessary. Pastors are not necessary. This is a major cause of angst for me. I want to be able to do something like prescribe medicine. I want a title that makes people think I'm an expert at something important. I want to be called something like Ph.D., M.D., or attorney-at-law. What I do is be a friend. It doesn't impress people and, frankly, it doesn't impress me. But it's what Jesus did. And friendship is a parable of the grace of God, so it delivers God.

Friendship isn't easy for me. My idea of the perfect evening is to do something with my family. My idea of a perfect day at work revolves around my books, my computer, walking, and praying. Alone stuff is what I do best, what I'm most comfortable doing. But in my mind, I see a door I need to knock on.

I have fewer ideas about how I'm supposed to be someone's friend than I have about any other task in the ministry. I don't know how friendship happens to me, and I don't know how to make it happen with other people. I've got a toolbox, though, and it's always open.

What is a pastor? To get a true picture, I boil things down and then peek inside the kettle after the steam is gone to see what's stuck on the bottom. When I cook down pastoral ministry, I see pastors bringing Jesus to people by being like Jesus. Jesus taught the Word, he prayed for people, he befriended people; and on his last night, to cap it off, he served the sacrament.

A pastor is a parable of Jesus Christ. Serving like Jesus served, pastors deliver something that they are not: Jesus.

"Whoever welcomes you, welcomes me" (Matt. 10:40). Serving as Jesus served means doing the simple things we see Jesus doing: teaching the Word, praying for people, being a friend, and serving the sacrament. But it's more than that. Being a parable of Jesus demands following Jesus' way: "If any want to become my followers, let them deny themselves and take up their cross and follow me" (Mark 8:34). This means love and humility—the abolition of personal ambition.

Learning this has changed how I feel about my work. Knowing that what I am called to do is a few simple things gives centrality of vision to my work. It's like having a round of lodgepole pine sitting straight up and square on a chopping block.

Eventually, Kathryn went into a nursing home. It was a happy thing. She was clean, well fed, and comfortable. Most of us worried about how she'd take it, but in time she adjusted well. The nursing staff was marvelous. She walked the halls a lot and talked with fellow residents.

Kathryn's close to 100 now. She talks about death with little or no apprehension and accepts help graciously. She is more confused about some things—like where she grew up and where her sister and niece live—but less confused about others.

"I was born and raised in a little hollow just across town," she says. "My family still lives there . . . they could come see me if they wanted. I don't know why they don't come see me."

Willa and I try to orient her a little, but nothing helps. We just listen. It feels like a long time.

"Kathryn, it's time to read the Scriptures, pray, and have the Lord's Supper," I say.

"Okay," she replies. She waits quietly. I read the Scriptures. "Yes, that's a good one," she says.

I pray—whatever comes to mind. Something happens. Suddenly we are located together, and God is with us. We aren't alone anymore, we don't wonder where we are anymore, and we don't wonder why people aren't visiting us; we are at home and well and all together. For an untimeable moment, we rest in the Sabbath arms of the communion of the saints mediated by the Holy Spirit of Jesus Christ, Lord of the church.

My eyes break open after the prayer, and all is peace. Kathryn is quiet, no longer alone; she is located in the presence of God. We serve the Lord's Supper as a stone altar stacked up to commemorate the place where God met us.

Upon rising to leave, I stoop over and give her a

hug. She reaches up and returns my embrace.

"I have charity for you, Kathryn," I say.

"Well, that's nice," she chuckles. "A person needs a lot of that." She smiles deeply, and her eyes look up at me with all the glistening of someone who can see.